THE RECORD OF
MURDERS
AND
OUTRAGES

CIVIL WAR AMERICA

Peter S. Carmichael, Caroline E. Janney,
and Aaron Sheehan-Dean, editors

This landmark series interprets broadly the history and culture of the Civil War era through the long nineteenth century and beyond. Drawing on diverse approaches and methods, the series publishes historical works that explore all aspects of the war, biographies of leading commanders, and tactical and campaign studies, along with select editions of primary sources. Together, these books shed new light on an era that remains central to our understanding of American and world history.

THE RECORD OF

MURDERS

AND

OUTRAGES

Racial Violence and the
FIGHT OVER TRUTH
at the Dawn of Reconstruction

WILLIAM A. BLAIR

THE UNIVERSITY OF NORTH CAROLINA PRESS

Chapel Hill

Designed by Jamison Cockerham
Set in Arno, Scala Sans, Cutright, and Irby
by codeMantra

Cover illustration: *Scenes in Memphis, during the Riot,* by Alfred R. Waud.
From *Harper's Weekly,* May 26, 1866. Courtesy Library of Congress.

Manufactured in the United States of America

The University of North Carolina Press has been a
member of the Green Press Initiative since 2003.

LIBRARY OF CONGRESS CATALOGING-IN-PUBLICATION DATA
Names: Blair, William Alan, author.
Title: The record of murders and outrages : racial violence and the
fight over truth at the dawn of Reconstruction / William A. Blair.
Other titles: Civil War America (Series)
Description: Chapel Hill : University of North Carolina Press, [2021] |
Series: Civil War America | Includes bibliographical references and index.
Identifiers: LCCN 2021003506 | ISBN 9781469663449
(cloth ; alk. paper) | ISBN 9781469663456
(paperback ; alk. paper) | ISBN 9781469663463 (ebook)
Subjects: LCSH: United States. Bureau of Refugees, Freedmen, and
Abandoned Lands—Records and correspondence. | Freedmen—Southern
States—History—19th century—Sources. | African Americans—Violence
against—Southern States—Sources. | Reconstruction (U.S. history,
1865–1877)—Public opinion. | United States—Race relations—History—
19th century. | United States—Politics and government—1865–1877.
Classification: LCC E185.2 .B55 2021 | DDC 973.8—dc23
LC record available at https://lccn.loc.gov/2021003506

CONTENTS

TABLES

THE RECORD OF
MURDERS
AND
OUTRAGES

INTRODUCTION

While working on research for another project some thirty years ago, I took a break from cranking microfilm in the Alderman Library at the University of Virginia. Walking through the stacks, I spotted reels from the National Archives containing material from the Bureau of Refugees, Freedmen, and Abandoned Lands, commonly called the Freedmen's Bureau. At the time, I thought the material might inform my thinking about the appropriate end point of my research, which potentially straddled the end of the Civil War and the early days of Reconstruction. Taking one reel back to my reader, I threaded the spool and stopped at the title page, which read, "Records Relating to Murders and Outrages."[1]

The title startled me. Such powerful words in a government record dating from that era made clear that its creators were reporting bona fide atrocities, and inclusion within the Freedmen's Bureau archives indicated that African Americans had been the targets. But who had originated the reports and for what purpose? Had they helped bring the perpetrators to justice? Or did the material represent another example of information gathered by a bureaucracy only to be filed and ignored in the bowels of government archives?

It turns out that the Records Relating to Murders and Outrages were central to one of the most important conflicts of the

Reconstruction era—a conflict that was, at its heart, a war over trustworthy information.

The thousands of pages that make up the records reveal that federal agents gathered intelligence to prove the pervasiveness of racial conflict and violent atrocities against freedpeople in the Reconstruction South. The moment was awash in debate and confusion, particularly about the accuracy of news that had begun to emanate out of the former Confederate states about such atrocities. In the first months after the end of the Civil War, disputes over information raged along partisan lines. Democrats and conservative Republicans accused Radicals in Congress of distorting the extent of criminal behavior perpetrated by Southerners. The critics alleged that Radicals fabricated or exaggerated the stories of violence in order to send the military into the South on a supposed mission of mercy that hid a baser motive—to expand the party's base through Black manhood suffrage. In a media landscape that was as partisan as the halls of government, Democrats and conservative Republicans refused to believe correspondents from opposing newspapers about lawlessness. Doubters also rejected the testimony from witnesses delivered before congressional committees under oath and denied the existence of the Ku Klux Klan.[2]

Even when confronted with seemingly hard evidence, critics dismissed the murders, rapes, assaults, and other outrages on Black people as either cultural or social conflicts rather than struggles over political power to maintain white supremacy. They claimed that if African Americans experienced crime, it was nothing more than the usual violence occurring everywhere in America, including between white people. They also claimed, without proof, that white people were more often the victims of outrages perpetrated by Black people.

In an effort to produce unmistakable evidence, officers of the Freedmen's Bureau stationed in Southern communities after the Civil War documented racial violence to show that former rebels persecuted freedpeople and white Republicans through terrorism. Without the knowledge of President Andrew Johnson, they began to collect the data and eventually leaked it to Radicals in the Senate.

Their efforts contradicted Johnson's policies and supported passage of legislation for military rule of the South.[3]

The records also make it clear that Black people laid their lives on the line to supply the documentation. White supremacists resented the Freedmen's Bureau in their communities and used all forms of intimidation, including murder, to prevent African Americans from testifying about the injustice they faced. Freedpeople encountered a law enforcement system stacked against them and civil courts that failed to prosecute the criminals who perpetrated acts against them. Because of this, Freedmen's Bureau officers estimated that they received news of only a fraction of the outrages committed against Black people.

The sacrifices that Black people endured to share their testimony of white atrocities made an impact. Military Reconstruction led to newly elected Republican governments in the South, which in turn adopted Black manhood suffrage. Those governments also ratified the Fourteenth Amendment, which empowered the federal government to protect individual liberties. The intelligence on violence gathered by the Freedmen's Bureau influenced other debates and policy formation. The monthly reports exposed the election intimidation that threatened newly registered Republican voters and put Georgia and Louisiana in the hands of Democrats. The information helped slow the timetable for readmission of states, especially Georgia.[4]

But the story behind this record also exposes how difficult it has been to overcome white disbelief of the scope of racist violence against Black people—not just at the time but for at least another century. African Americans continued to bear witness to the violence and repression their communities suffered, but they were not joined by the white historical establishment until the 1960s, when scholars increasingly saw the truth about violence revealed in the archive. By the 1980s, historians using the reports of outrages produced important studies of Reconstruction violence. Nearly every historian of Reconstruction since has consulted the Freedmen's Bureau record for its catalog of white atrocities. Familiarity with the archival material has been aided by the Freedmen and Southern Society Project at the University of Maryland and an internet project, the Freedmen's Bureau Online, which has reproduced a fairly extensive sampling of the murders and outrages material. In the past few decades, studies have tapped this documentation of lawlessness to reveal, among other things, the sexual assaults on Black women, the problems of military occupation after the Civil War, the central role of violence in U.S. history, and the trauma that left its mark on survivors.[5]

None of this remarkable outpouring of books, however, has told the story of the record itself—its creation and the role it played in Reconstruction and beyond. Nor have we appreciated sufficiently enough how this effort to collect data on racial violence became part of the bureau's mission, one instituted for a deliberate policy objective that then continued—even if the execution was hampered because of the lack of resources for the officers, the obstacles they faced from Southern whites, and the dangers Black people endured to make their problems known.

The microfilm reel containing Virginia's conflict that I encountered so many years ago represented only the tip of the iceberg. Monthly reports of atrocities by bureau officers became common by January 1867. The officers also collated what they could from earlier information, which was of course sporadic and imperfect. And the reporting continued month by month until the bulk of officers were largely withdrawn from the South after the end of 1868. The product of this labor today fills nine microfilm reels cataloging violence in eight states and the District of Columbia.[6]

Although the collection records between 5,000 and 6,000 crimes against individuals, it does not tally all the lives lost or describe the full scope of the violence endured. It does reveal, however, that lawlessness almost immediately gripped the former Confederacy, and it developed into overt political terrorism as African Americans gained the vote through military occupation in 1867.[7] The record also shines a bright light on rural violence, which has been less systematically explored in the syntheses on Reconstruction and can be overshadowed by the more accessible reporting of events in cities and towns. Thanks to the reports gathered by the Freedmen's Bureau, we can begin to see beyond well-known massacres in Memphis and New

Orleans in 1866 and into the violence committed by night riders, the Ku Klux Klan, and political terrorists in the countryside.[8]

Despite the racial violence that historians have exposed over the past several decades, public impressions of Reconstruction may yet remain more greatly influenced by those who rejected the lawlessness as part of this history. Over the years, movies such as *The Birth of a Nation* and *Gone with the Wind*, popular books, and textbooks joined with biased academic histories to indoctrinate Americans with erroneous ideas about law and order in the post–Civil War South. Concerns remain about the lack of public knowledge of the era—especially for how, in the words of the Equal Justice Initiative, the deadly attacks in the first years of freedom paved the way for the later era of racial terrorism that employed lynching to solidify Jim Crow policies and practices. The extent of atrocities has remained imperfectly represented in public memory.[9] The proof of what really happened lies in the Records Relating to Murders and Outrages.

1

THE BATTLE
FOR CREDIBILITY

On February 19, 1867, Senator Henry Wilson of Massachusetts presented to his colleagues a chilling list of atrocities that had been committed against Black people in the conquered South. As chair of the Military Affairs Committee, he supplied evidence that the Civil Rights Act of 1866 was not being enforced and argued that the North needed to enact martial law to protect white and Black loyalists. Reading from "a little book," the senator announced that 375 freedmen had been murdered from April to December 1866. Another 556 were the victims of "outrages," a term for assaults, fraud, arson, robbery, rape, and other crimes. He broke down the violence by states, indicating widespread lawlessness while showing Texas as an epicenter for the tremors rocking the former Confederacy. Wherever possible, he named the perpetrators and victims.[1] Wilson's data represented a change in how Radical Republicans in the Senate supported their arguments for military control of the South. Instead of referring to private letters from anonymous people or accounts from the partisan press, the senator relied on the Freedmen's Bureau for the specific details of criminal behavior. He did so to counter the opposition's tendency to dismiss news of atrocities as false.

For roughly a year and a half after the end of the Civil War, Republicans had tried to convince the nation that former Confederates

were employing egregious acts of violence to maintain white supremacy and limit the changes wrought by the Union victory. But their
efforts faced an uphill fight against racism in a divisive partisan climate. Democrats and some Republicans opposed those who sought
to remake the nation's racial order and refused to accept the reports
of atrocities committed against Black people. Republican senator
James R. Doolittle of Wisconsin was typical. A conservative who
started out his political career as a Democrat, he insisted that fellow
Republicans exaggerated the situation to discredit Southern governments. He called the reports of violence "absolutely, unqualifiedly,
and wickedly false." On the other side of the debate, Radical Republicans argued that the Johnson administration misrepresented information on outrages, understating them so that Northern Democrats
could quickly restore their alliance in a national party with Southern
whites. Massachusetts senator Charles Sumner, a leading Radical,
just months after the war accused no less than the president of the
United States of "whitewashing" news of atrocities.[2]

The political struggles over Reconstruction prominently featured
arguments over the truth behind information. Republicans believed
that racial violence presented an increasing problem. And yet no one
had reliable data on the extent of atrocities, which left matters open
for debate. Did the United States need to send troops into the former
Confederacy to try to keep the peace as they forced on the South ratification of the Fourteenth Amendment and suffrage for Black men?
Or were the rebels, as the Johnson administration alleged, acquiesc-
ing in the terms of reunion? Northern opinion sharply divided over
whether the violence existed to the degree that demanded military
intervention. News from correspondents in the South invariably fell
along partisan lines, supporting the arguments of either side. Radical
Republicans eventually reached out to the U.S. military stationed
in the South to prove that they had their fingers on the pulse of the
situation.

Wilson's information came not from newspapers or anecdotal
rumor but from a network of military officers and African Americans who bore witness to the atrocities committed by former rebels.
The collaboration started at the grassroots level, linking freedpeople

and local officers of the Freedmen's Bureau. The chain extended to prominent military officers, including Ulysses S. Grant, the general-in-chief of the army, and Gen. Oliver Otis Howard, the commissioner of the Freedmen's Bureau, all the way to Secretary of War Edwin Stanton, who leaked it to the Senate. Together, these hands created a government collection known as the Records Relating to Murders and Outrages.

Peace left unresolved questions about the rebels: whether they had accepted the verdict of war about slavery and secession, whether they wished to rejoin the Union as law-abiding citizens, and whether they could live harmoniously with newly freed African Americans. Uncertainty existed about what Northerners called the "Southern feeling," a shorthand for whether white Confederates had accepted federal authority. Abolitionists, Radical Republicans, and Northern Black people heard rumors that emancipation had escalated racial hostilities. Courts generally prohibited Black testimony against white people. It seemed important to Radicals that Black men voted not only because it was right but also because it gave them influence with state governments to protect their civil rights and personal well-being. Black manhood suffrage, supporters maintained, ensured that the old rebel element did not resume positions of power uncontested.

The ability of Southern whites to influence national affairs represented a real concern for Republicans. With their civic rights restored, former Confederates ironically gained political power through defeat. The Constitution had counted slaves as three-fifths of a person for determining representation in Congress. With emancipation, however, that rule no longer applied as Black people, now free, factored as full persons for calculating apportionment, causing the South to gain seats in Congress. If African American men remained disenfranchised, Black people thus augmented the national influence of former rebels, without having a voice in government. Robert Dale Owen, a noted Northern social reformer, fretted about this problem in a public letter. The result could be administration of the "secession portion of the Union, through the agency of its enemies." Owen characterized the national attachment of these leaders as no more than "lip-loyal."[3] Republicans understood that the balance of national power could easily tip back toward Democrats supported by the enemy who had cost so many Northern lives.

In this atmosphere, both sides of policy debates viewed the other as using false rhetoric to mask underlying attempts to gain political advantage. Democrats especially became adroit at branding reports of violence as "cruel falsehoods of certain press correspondents" who misrepresented Southern whites for political and personal interests.[4] They painted a portrait of compliant enemies who accepted defeat, recognized the reality of emancipation, and wished to move on with their lives in peace. They rejected as baseless the Republican newspaper stories about persecution of white Unionists and freedpeople. To them, the violence that existed represented nothing more than what occurred throughout the nation.

Republicans and newspaper correspondents had their doubts. Immediately after the war, however, many Northerners were uncertain about the "Southern feeling." A hunger existed to know a range of news about former Confederates: the conditions of battlefields, the extent of destruction, the chances of economic recovery, and whether the war spirit still smoldered. Noncombatants had little direct exposure to the rebels during the war, and citizens in much of the country—predominantly rural and living in worlds often circumscribed by neighborhoods—had likely never been in the South. By the summer of 1865, various correspondents toured the region, writers looking to satisfy the demand of a Northern populace eager to learn about the people who had resisted them so fiercely for four long years. Invariably, these reports featured the writer's sense of the rebels' willingness to comply with the verdict of the war. The answer was mixed. One such account noted that in Charlestown, West Virginia—where Southerners had executed John Brown for his raid on Harpers Ferry—the people remained rebels and that the war feeling was "like a burning bush with a wet blanket wrapped around it." To erupt anew, the fire simply needed more air.[5]

Sheer happenstance placed a federal agency in the position of gathering intelligence on the "Southern feeling." Short for the Bureau of Refugees, Freedmen, and Abandoned Lands, the Freedmen's Bureau served as a key source for reporting on conditions within the South. It did not begin with such a mission. Established in March 1865, the bureau aided the transition of African Americans from slavery to freedom. One of the first national social welfare agencies, the bureau fell under the auspices of the War Department and placed military officers in communities throughout the defeated Confederacy and in the border states. Besides overseeing the subsistence, education, work contracts, and health of freedpeople, officers also had responsibility for ensuring that justice was accomplished when civil authorities failed to act. This much had been outlined in Circular No. 5 of May 1865, which established procedures for assistant commissioners in charge of states. The agency, however, had not been given an official charge of supplying information that might affect the political situation. That came later.[6]

Some officers of the bureau sent to Washington news of horrible things that happened under their jurisdiction. They could not help but notice the wrongdoing around them. It often began with planters—now called employers—who failed to live up to the terms of free labor and refused to either make or honor contracts. Some, like a man in Virginia who threatened his former slaves, now freed, with death if they left and dared bureau officers to interfere. In this case, a military guard freed some of the former slaves but ran into an ambush while trying to reach others.[7] This and other descriptions of coercion crept into the correspondence that made its way up from sub-assistant commissioners stationed in counties to the assistant commissioners in charge of states and then to Commissioner O. O. Howard, who supervised the bureau from Washington. The reporting was not as consistent as it later became. Officers did not follow a format, and they may or may not have indicated the particulars of outbreaks. As often as not, newspapers and politicians used the reports by military officers that described outrages in a general fashion, speaking of areas of concern rather than offering individual details.

Still, enough information flowed to the North from various sources to put Republican congressmen on alert that all was not well in the region. Reports came via newspaper clipping services—the exchanges that shared items reproduced verbatim from cooperating organs. Others came from private individuals, some of whom were Northerners hoping to settle in the region but feared for their lives. And then there was the Freedmen's Bureau, whose communications and circulars also appeared in newspaper columns. Through these various means, Republicans and sympathizers of freedpeople learned distressing news about the treatment of Black people in the South.

Andrew Johnson also wanted to know more about conditions in the South. Throughout 1865 he sent emissaries there to report on what they found. Among the first was Carl Schurz, former Union general and Radical Republican.[8] During a meeting in Washington about a month after the war, Schurz told the president that the government needed clarity about the Southern mood and someone to advise the administration in this capacity. Johnson had complained about the lack of reliable information and "being always obliged to act in the dark." The president wanted to see how Southern whites embraced his policies that disenfranchised Confederate political and military leaders, as well as rich people worth more than $20,000. This was early in the process— before he employed widespread use of the pardon power that eliminated most political disabilities, allowing for a speedy reunion with traitors. He also was being pressured by the Radicals to promote Black manhood suffrage and probably wanted to hold them off by confirming his sense that good relations existed between whites and the freedpeople.[9]

Schurz warmed to the job as he recognized that his mission would undercut the president's ability to say that he had crafted policies based on incomplete information. Stanton also encouraged him to assume the task, stressing its importance. Schurz remained in contact throughout his tour with Charles Sumner, who urged the ex-general not only to publish a report but also to deliver speeches on his findings. They hoped to pressure the president into adopting their position.[10]

While still in the South, Schurz tipped his hand about the nature of his forthcoming report. In five letters to the *Boston Advertiser* between July and August, he portrayed Southern whites in South

Carolina and Georgia as incapable of functioning within a free labor system that required contracts and the autonomy of laborers to enter such relations. Southern whites, he wrote, doubted that the freedpeople would work without physical coercion. Violence did not dominate Schurz's letters, but he did describe discord over a Black procession, and he depicted the region around Atlanta as rife with "negro-shooting." He considered the former Confederacy unfit for resuming normal political relations and predicted that the underlying tensions promised that extensive violence lay ahead as federal troops withdrew.[11]

The Democratic press characterized these reports, whether from Schurz or others, as fraudulent—designed to cover ulterior motives. The *Albany Argus* ran the headline "Misrepresenting the South," claiming that "agitators" lied about Southern people's resistance because the accusers intended to "keep alive sectional hatred, and drive the people into extreme measures." When held to scrutiny, the writer maintained, the yarns proved to be "manufactured out of whole cloth to accomplish a wicked purpose."[12] The *Alexandria Gazette* said Schurz's letters were "calculated to do more injury than the Schurz mission is likely to do good." It criticized him for failing to perform his mission quietly and for instead leaking his material to the public before reporting to the War Department. Former postmaster general Montgomery Blair was more pointed in charging "Stanton & Co." with employing "swarms of hireling writers to misrepresent the South." He considered Schurz "one of Stanton's hireling writers" who tried to undermine the policy of the president.[13]

To head off the damage expected from Schurz's final report, Johnson ordered Ulysses S. Grant to file an assessment of the Southern feeling. Somewhat reluctantly, Grant began the journey in late November and endured a superficial trip that featured only five days of investigation. Although he encountered Black people who cheered him along the way, he spent most of his time with white elites who feted him as they reassured him that the rebellion had ended and that they now tried to make the best of the situation. Grant did not have his heart in this visit. He made a perfunctory tour that fulfilled his duty but wanted to return home to his family as quickly as possible. In a letter to his wife, he foreshadowed his report by saying, "all seem pleasant and at least towards me, to and I thinks towards the Government, to enter faithfully upon a course to restore harmony between the sections."[14]

As the Thirty-Ninth Congress convened in Washington in December 1865, a number of controversial elements came together that raised the ante on assessing the sentiments of the rebels. The first came with the decision to admit Southern representatives elected through new governments organized according to Johnson's leniency. Most of the elections had restored to power the old guard. The South sent to Congress four Confederate generals, five colonels, and the vice president of the Confederacy.[15] The Republican-dominated Congress refused to seat the newcomers. Meanwhile, new state governments in the readmitted states enacted Black Codes, which restricted African Americans' travel, employment, meetings, and other freedoms while denying them the right to vote, to testify in court, or to serve on juries. To many in the North, it looked like the re-creation of slavery—and as if the rebels were winning the peace.

At the same time, Republicans formed a committee consisting of fifteen members (nine from the House, six from the Senate) to conduct its own investigation into Southern conditions. They could not have sent a clearer message of their mistrust of the president. All told, Congress called 144 persons to Washington, including former Confederate general Robert E. Lee. The panel probed whether the former rebels had accepted national authority. Congressmen also asked about the treatment of freedpeople and white Unionists. The inquiry concluded that without protection by the military, the freedpeople could not live safely, nor could "Union men, whether of northern or southern origin." The committee added, "This deep-seated prejudice against color is assiduously cultivated by the public journals, and leads to acts of cruelty, oppression, and murder, which the local authorities are at no pains to prevent or punish." To address this problem, the committee framed recommendations that became the basis for the Fourteenth Amendment to the Constitution, which enabled the federal government to enforce equal protection under the laws.[16]

Small wonder that on December 19, the reports of Schurz and Grant—introduced officially to Congress by an overview from the president—sparked inflammatory debate that revealed the divide between the parties over how to describe the attitudes and actions of former rebels, especially as they concerned the ability of white Unionists and Black people to live their lives in peace. Johnson asserted that former Confederates had reorganized state governments and yielded to the laws of the United States "with more willingness and greater promptitude than, under the circumstances, could reasonably have been anticipated," a position spread throughout the country by friendly newspapers. Moreover, with the exception of Mississippi, the governments had ratified the Thirteenth Amendment that ended slavery. As for violence, Johnson admitted that some disorder occasionally occurred but added that "these are local in character, not frequent in occurrence, and are rapidly disappearing as the authority of civil law is extended and sustained."[17]

Republicans embraced Schurz's report, which countered the president's claims with evidence spanning more than 100 pages, divided roughly equally between the general's text and supporting documents. Although Schurz conceded that the rebellion was largely over—that no fighting threatened between conventional armies—hatred between the sections had not abated. He heard enmity expressed toward Union soldiers. Some had been shot, but more were vilified as "Yankees" and "the enemy." He feared the rapid return to power of men who only recently had engaged in a bitter war against the United States. Turning against Johnson his own phrase about punishing treason, Schurz wrote, "Treason does, under existing circumstances, not appear odious in the south. The people are not impressed with any sense of its criminality."[18]

When describing the condition of the freedpeople, Schurz diverged significantly from the president. The military encountered atrocities. He quoted Brig. Gen. Francis Fessenden in South Carolina, who described persecution manifested by white people upon African Americans. "They are shot and abused, outside the immediate protection of our forces," he wrote, "*by men who announce their determination to take the law into their own hands, in defiance of our authority.*" Offering an oft-repeated prescription by military officers in the South, Fessenden believed that protection of freedpeople and punishment of rebellious individuals depended upon having "this country pretty thickly settled with soldiers." In the documents he furnished, Schurz included many from the Freedmen's Bureau. One told of the killing of a woman who tried to stop the whipping of her son. In another instance in Mississippi, assailants stripped a woman, tied her to a tree, and whipped her. The same report indicated that someone had murdered five freedmen. No one said it at the time, but the documents proved the ability of the bureau in gathering information on violence. It was a harbinger of things to come.[19]

For a person with today's sensibilities, it is difficult not to wince at Grant's depiction in his report of Black people and the Freedmen's Bureau. He confessed, "I did not give the operations of the Freedmen's Bureau that attention I would have done if more time had been at my disposal," yet this did not prevent him from criticizing the organization and claiming that Black people were unready for freedom. He spent more time warning about the potential problems with Black people and the white agents who aided in their transition than he did analyzing the rebels. Despite this, Grant saw the need for the bureau to continue to exist as a protection for Black people.[20]

In the debate over Schurz's report, Charles Sumner rose to the defense of the observations. Johnson had sent his overall assessment packaged with Grant's letter. Schurz's report came separately, and it was unclear to Sumner if it had been annexed with the other material. (It apparently had not been printed yet.) Assured that it was, he wanted it read aloud, which drew protests even from sympathizers because of the report's length. Sumner reminded colleagues that the report on conditions in Kansas in the 1850s had been read word for word and that the questions before the country now were even more important. Then he cast doubt on Johnson's veracity. "We have a message from the President which is like the whitewashing message of Franklin Pierce with regard to the enormities in Kansas," he said, adding, "That is its parallel."[21]

Senator Reverdy Johnson, a Democrat from Maryland, objected. He "did not expect to hear any assault, direct or indirect, upon the President at this time" and denied that the president had tried to whitewash anything. He considered Johnson's assessments fairly stated and worth the Senate's attention. Taking a stronger approach, Senator James R. Doolittle from Wisconsin, a fellow Republican, urged Sumner to modify his comments or retract them. Instead, Sumner doubled down, saying that the country now had eleven Kansases, which made the current circumstances worse than the 1850s. Doolittle continued to upbraid Sumner for calling the president a liar.[22]

The dispute flowed over into the next day's session, with Sumner marshaling evidence to prove the president's representation wrong. The senator referenced reports from more than twenty witnesses in the South, often quoting extensively from their descriptions of violence. In sum, according to Sumner, they showed planters as exhibiting a cruel, remorseless, and vindictive spirit against the freedpeople, with outrages committed especially in areas without Union soldiers.[23]

But there was a problem with the nature of Sumner's evidence. He identified the authorship of less than a handful of the letters he had received. His listeners likely knew the "North Carolina newspaper" that he referred to without naming it, as well as his mention of an unidentified Southern governor. And he revealed the name of a cotton agent who traveled through the rebel states. But the vast majority of his information came from what he called "private letters," whose authors remained unstated. This was not unusual. Senators often did this, citing protection of an individual from possible persecution or the reluctance to put a person into an indelicate position without the writer's permission. However, the intense partisan warfare left such an approach a ready target for dismissal.

Senator Willard Saulsbury, a Democrat from Delaware, joined with Republican senator Edgar Cowan of Pennsylvania to suggest that the reports either had been falsified or written by men whose word would not be taken seriously if their identities were known. Saulsbury alleged that the real concern by Republicans was the

Democratic Party's opportunity to return to power—a reference to the refusal to seat Southern representatives based on continuing disorder in the South. Cowan was even more antagonistic, showing fissures among the Republicans as he asked whether the news of violence came from people furnishing "a series of *ex parte* statements made up by anonymous letter-writers, people who are down there more than likely stealing cotton, people who are down there in the enjoyment of place and power, people who are interested that the disturbed condition of things which exists there now shall always continue because they make profit of it?" He added that one man in 10,000 may have committed brutality against a freed person, which opponents then made representative of the 9,999 others. He hinted that Sumner deviously could have sent his own emissaries into the South to gather evidence from "knaves and fools and discontented." When Sumner denied that he read from anonymous letters (he knew who had written them), Cowan blurted out, "They are anonymous so far as we are concerned: and I commend the Senator's prudence in keeping the names of their writers from the public, because I have no doubt that if their names were known they would not be considered of much importance."[24]

Sumner remained a lightning rod for criticism that he supposedly manufactured lies in letters that he wrote himself, passing them off as the opinions of unnamed witnesses. More than a year later during a different political controversy, a Cincinnati writer cautioned readers not to trust Republicans even if they took an oath when testifying before legislative bodies. Such oaths had no moral binding, the writer asserted, because the Republicans considered them part of a political investigation, giving them a license to lie. The newspaper took on Sumner more directly with biting commentary, claiming that he "can sit in his room and write letters to himself purporting to come from loyalists in the South giving terrible pictures of murders and outrages by rebels on white and Black loyalists, and produce the same letters before the Senate as genuine productions—withholding the names of the alleged writers." In other words, he had been an habitual forgerer.[25]

Consequently, as 1865 came to a close, just who told the truth about conditions within the South—a Radical like Schurz, a moderate like Grant, or a conservative like Johnson—could seem debatable. To resolve the uncertainty, Republicans looked for more authoritative information to justify their eventual policy to establish military rule in the former Confederacy. The next year brought numerous examples as the army, the Freedmen's Bureau, and the Radicals in Congress refined their means of reporting on atrocities.

Not long after the dispute over his report, Grant showed signs of doubting his position. He apparently said as much to Schurz, who told his wife, "Grant feels very bad about his thoughtless move and has openly expressed his regrets for what he has done."[26] It is not clear what triggered his next move shortly after the report hit Congress—whether the general initiated the action based on his changing attitudes or answered a request from the president to gather better intelligence of Southern feelings. In any event, Grant sought details of violence. On Christmas Day, he telegraphed generals in command of military departments in the former Confederacy to report "all known outrages occurring within your command since the surrender of the rebel Armies, committed by white people against the Blacks, and the reverse." He wanted this information as soon as possible.[27]

Reports from the field proved that African Americans needed protection. His subordinates had compiled a table organized by military departments of assaults, larceny, murders, disorderly conduct, and drunkenness. At the time, officers did not supply the dates of incidents, locations of crimes, or names of victims and perpetrators that became typical in Freedmen's Bureau reporting. Yet the numbers were revealing. Officers had scraped together from unknown sources that forty-four African Americans had died at the hands of white people. More significantly, not one Black person had killed a white person. White people also had instigated a little more than 60 percent of all assaults, meaning the violence was decidedly one-sided. Grant forwarded the details to President Johnson without comment; it is unclear whether he received a response or whether the information found a use.[28]

The statistics on murders seem low for a span of roughly eight months, but the information had been patched together quickly and probably with little input from the Freedmen's Bureau. And the information included totals for only five states—hardly a complete picture. The data had been funneled through military departmental commands, which at the time featured a reporting stream and chain of command separate from the bureau. Military commanders sent information directly to Grant. Freedmen's Bureau information, meanwhile, flowed to Commissioner Howard and then on to Secretary Stanton, bypassing the general-in-chief. Grant hated this command structure for its lack of efficiency and for allowing too much independence to bureau agents. In his letter to Johnson, he singled out a lack of discipline among Freedmen's Bureau agents, who operated independently without answering to the military commander in a region.[29] He eventually consolidated the command structure, but the circumstances meant that his tally of murders understated the outrages—especially since neither the army commanders nor the bureau had yet adopted the habit of collecting the data.

Always eager to serve his superior officer, Howard immediately ordered tours by Freedmen's Bureau personnel throughout the former Confederacy to correct the "evils" Grant had mentioned. The responses appeared within a government document requested by Congress in March 1866 to bolster arguments for continuing the Freedmen's Bureau, which had a one-year term requiring annual renewal. To the surprise of many, Johnson had vetoed the legislation to continue the agency, proclaiming it an unconstitutional overreach of military authority by establishing army agents who interceded in contracts and even minor court actions. The president said the war had ended; peace reigned. Citing liberal principles of economics, he claimed that competition among planters for the labor of freedpeople kept workers safe and enabled them to enter or leave contracts voluntarily. They enjoyed the freedom to move to escape hostilities. This was largely untrue, though, a point underscored by the information that came from agents and inspectors unleashed by

Grant's criticism. Even though they had not been charged to collect the news, the inspectors saw it there for the taking.

In the document, agents told of outrages virtually everywhere, yet the most detailed accounts came from Kentucky. Clinton B. Fisk, assistant commissioner, wrote, "There are some of the *meanest*[,] *unsubjugated* and *unreconstructed, rascally rebellious revolutionists* in Kentucky that curse the soil of the country." He said that despite the Thirteenth Amendment, some planters claimed slavery was not dead, while others expected compensation for their losses. P. Bonesteel, a special inspector for Kentucky and Tennessee, corroborated the meanness as he reported twenty-three beatings and whippings, four beatings and shootings, two robberies with shootings, three other robberies, five men shot and killed, two shot and wounded, four men beaten to death, one beaten and "roasted," three women raped, two men and families beaten and driven from their homes, and two arsons. Authorities had arrested only one suspect, who was released on light bail and remained at large without trial. In another case, a bureau agent tried to arrest two men who robbed a Black man, shot him in the head, and then raped his wife, but a county judge released the assailants, claiming the bureau had no legal jurisdiction in Kentucky.[30]

The reporting provides several takeaways. First, both Fisk and Bonesteel considered the assaults by white people on African Americans as purposeful and targeted, rather than spontaneous and emotional. Fisk stressed, "The entire opposition is political, a warfare waged against *loyalty, freedom,* and *justice.*" He said planters committed atrocities on Black veterans who had recently mustered out of service. Similarly, Bonesteel noted that of the victims in his account, twelve had been Union soldiers and three were wives of Union veterans. Political terrorism grew more evident within a couple of years, but it was certainly present even this early.[31] Second, communiqués from Washington with instructions to assistant commissioners about the monthly reports they needed to file did not, at this time, ask officials to track atrocities. It took more than a year for this to become standard practice. Reporting resulted from the natural inclination of the officers on the ground.[32]

Finally, Bonesteel supplied a record that showed the potential for cataloging outrages. He was ahead of his time in jotting down names of assailants and victims, supplying dates and localities for crimes, and following incidents through to their inevitable lack of justice by local authorities. He pursued this with a professionalism beyond the norm, even for later practice. He took evidence only under oath, backed by affidavits attesting to the authenticity of accounts. And then he transmitted the information from depositions that showed the more extreme cases of cruelty. While his format anticipated in its details the reporting that the Freedmen's Bureau eventually adopted, he remained extraordinary in his attention to legal formalities.[33]

Grant and Howard, whose distaste was growing for the lawlessness the military encountered, fought to curb atrocities that smacked the country in the face. During the year, violence in the South rose wherever one looked. Freedpeople bore the heaviest toll. A shooting between white police and Black soldiers recently mustered out of the Union army led to a rampage through Black neighborhoods in Memphis. The killings over the course of May 1–3 resulted in two whites and forty-six Blacks killed and the rape of Black women. Federal troops were needed to restore order in the city. At the end of July, another massacre of Black people occurred in New Orleans resulting in another forty-four dead.

These horrors took place after Congress had enacted a Civil Rights Act in March 1866 that empowered the executive branch to ensure equal application of the law. Senator Lyman Trumbull, a moderate Republican from Illinois, had taken the lead on this initiative, which gathered legal ideas that eventually became entrenched in the Fourteenth Amendment of the Constitution. The violence repulsed many moderates, causing them to support greater use of federal powers. Yet the Johnson administration did little to enforce the law.

Newspapers spread the stories of violence in Memphis and New Orleans across the country, and scholars have made the massacres part of the canon of Reconstruction histories. They were well known then and remain so today. But the Freedmen's Bureau representatives increasingly understood that, as awful as the massacres were, they represented only a partial story. In rural areas and small towns, bureau officers encountered a steady drumbeat of assaults, murders, and other crimes. While featuring Black Americans most prominently, white Unionists were also vulnerable. And so were the white soldiers and agents of the Freedmen's Bureau.

Assassinations of Freedmen's Bureau agents and threats against officers of the law made an impression on Grant, inching him toward an all-out break with the president in matters concerning violence. A lieutenant in the Freedmen's Bureau who was walking along a street in Grenada, Mississippi, sustained a fatal wound from three shots inflicted on him by a white man who stepped out from an alley. As the officer died, he supplied a description of the murderer, but civil authorities did nothing to apprehend the individual. Grant also learned of the wounding of a bureau agent in Thomasville, Georgia. The officer had fined a man for "unmercifully" beating a freedman he employed. The soldier survived the assassination attempt. In a third instance, Commissioner Howard said a white man shot down a freedman near Leesburg, Virginia, but authorities were afraid to step in. The sheriff wished that military authorities would take the case off his hands. This civilian officer of the law feared for his life. "The simple issuing of an order by yourself," Howard told Grant, "would go far to prevent the attacks upon officers of the Government on duty."[34]

In response to this and the general unrest, Grant issued General Orders No. 44 on July 6, 1866, authorizing department, district, and post commanders to arrest persons who committed crimes against officers and agents. His desire to ensure the safety of people under his charge was understandable, but he went much further in trying to curb the violence. His orders included protection of "citizens and inhabitants"—regardless of color—who suffered from outrages that local officials failed to investigate and prosecute.[35]

This was a bold move that allowed for military intervention in civilian affairs, giving officers on the ground the discretion to take such action on their own. Military officers like Maj. Gen. George Thomas in Tennessee made use of the new powers. In one case, where a policeman provoked a Union soldier into a quarrel so he could shoot the man dead, Thomas made an arrest. He realized, however, that opposition among local white people made a solution for such cases nearly impossible. In this instance, the white community closed ranks to spin a narrative that the killing had resulted from a police officer using appropriate force in the line of duty. It was unlikely that civil courts would prosecute.[36]

The order, though, showed that Grant understood what was happening in the South and that he committed the army to actions that the president would not. In fact, Johnson had proclaimed on April 2, 1866, that the insurrection had ended in the former states of the Confederacy, excepting Texas. The proclamation recognized the restoration of civil authority, which constricted the military's ability to intercede in matters involving criminal behavior. But Grant's order contradicted the president's assessment of the situation and prodded soldiers to do whatever they could when facing outrages, including alerting superiors and political leaders to the difficulties of pacifying the rebel South.

Even though reporting had not been systematic, the public learned about reports of violence from Freedmen's Bureau officers as sympathetic newspapers picked up and reproduced news of atrocities, sometimes verbatim from documents coming from personnel in the field. A Boston newspaper indicated that a general had reported to Commissioner Howard that Union men in Texas "are trembling for their lives." Maltreatment of the freedpeople was on the rise. Murderers and assassins who went unpunished now molded the political future of the state.[37] An account of atrocities committed in Georgia estimated that 300 African Americans had been killed between December 1865 and December 1866. The newspaper expressed its indignation in italics: *"It would be just as easy to get a jury in the State of New-York to convict a person of manslaughter for shooting a mad dog, as to get a jury of Rebels to find a Rebel guilty upon a charge of killing a negro."*[38]

Yet denial of the violence also continued, vexing people who knew the truth. The situation caused the assistant commissioner of the Freedmen's Bureau in charge of Georgia, Brig. Gen. Davis Tillson, to resort to a more direct method to spread the news: he published a public letter in newspapers. Such action underscored how seriously he took the matter. He was one of the more conservative officers in the bureau, which makes his statement more remarkable. He recounted violence occurring below Atlanta in Henry County, where a gang had been whipping, robbing, and killing freedpeople, driving them from plantations. The only activity that local law enforcement officials demonstrated in these matters was to release prisoners arrested by the bureau. Why Tillson resorted to a public letter became clear toward the end of his epistle: he was trying to overcome the allegations that the military acted in "an oppressive, tyrannical manner, without due investigation of knowledge of the facts."[39] He fought the impression that the Freedmen's Bureau overreacted to uncorroborated information out of bias.

What accounts for this seeming irrationality against accepting atrocities as happening? What caused Democrats in particular, and some independent-minded people, to discredit accounts attributed to soldiers and visitors to the South that the freedpeople and white loyalists were under consistent, vicious assault without recourse to the law?

Racism underlaid much of the blindness, which partisanship employed in ways that fanned and perpetuated mistrust. The parties played loose with the truth whenever trying to impugn the motives of the opposing side. The tactic was a standard part of the political culture in an era when newspapers made no pretense of objectivity but served as party organs to mobilize the electorate and distribute ballots for voting. Information about conditions in the South did not come from immediate images or visual elements—such as the television coverage in the 1950s and 1960s that brought the horrors of white backlash against civil rights protesters into American living rooms, or the video captures of racial violence that have done the same more recently. Instead, reports of violence filtered through textual sources known to be created by the parties for prejudicial purposes. Exaggeration was part and parcel of the business of journalists.

Additionally, Radical Republicans were not well loved, even by some members of their own party, raising suspicions that they misrepresented facts. They could seem self-righteous and unwilling to compromise on policies like Black suffrage that were ahead of the popular curve. And according to their critics, they fabricated stories.

Rumors abounded in the Republican press of outrageous atrocities committed that had no corroboration: a Georgia doctor sawed off the legs of a freedman to prevent him from leaving; Alabama officials supposedly found 133 Black bodies in the woods; two white men reportedly stretched a Black man across a log to chop off his head. An Illinois newspaper argued that these "pestilent lies" had traversed the country by telegraph but then had been discredited by further evidence.[40]

Capturing this mood was an item in the *New York Times* of August 1866 that bore the headline "The Falsehood and Exaggeration of the Radical Press." The *Times* was a Republican newspaper that supported the Lincoln administration during the war, including his emancipation of slaves as a war measure. Yet here it was, criticizing Radicals for producing erroneous information that fostered "anger and estrangement" between North and South so they could "ride into power on the strength of a pretended sympathy with the negro." Not a week went by, it proclaimed, without tidings of an ex-Union soldier slain in his bed somewhere in Georgia, or a Black man losing his life in a street brawl, the origin of which "we know nothing." Then came the Radical cries for imposing martial law and declaring "the Freedmen's Bureau as a saving agency between white wolves and black lambs."[41]

How frustrating for the people in the army like Howard and Grant who knew the violence happened, and yet nothing seemed to convince the naysayers—including some organs aligned with the Republican Party like the *Times*. Even with all of the evidence supplied by military officers, by newspaper correspondents, by travelers in the South, and by arguments on the floor of Congress, the notion persisted among opponents of the Radicals that the demand for turning the military into a national police force was based on a fiction. The president did not help matters; he preached that leniency worked and that ex-Confederates treated the freedpeople well. How could military officers convince even skeptical, moderate Republicans that all was not right in the South?

Howard understood the challenge involved in the fight for credibility. It was a problem he faced in defending the Freedmen's Bureau against its critics as he fought for annual renewal from Congress. In August 1866 he wrote Congressman Roswell Hart of New York a public letter in which he expressed frustration at how to convince the public about the necessity of continuing the bureau. He recognized the difficulty of finding a delicate balance in presenting information. "If I deal entirely with statistics," he noted, "the public are apt to wander through long tabular statements without comprehending their relation to the objects to be presented. If I fail to present facts and figures, and deal in generalities, I incur the displeasure of a large class of people who ask for such proof of results." How should he solve this dilemma? "I shall aim to group general statements with statistics in such a manner as to give a clear idea of the Bureau's work."[42]

The combination of general statements with statistics became an important shift in how the bureau went about its task of documenting atrocities. Beginning in September 1866, Howard started by tracking more systematically the murders committed against freedpeople. A circular went out on September 24 ordering assistant commissioners "to report, without giving the names of persons concerned, the number of murders that have occurred in your district where freedmen have been victims, or parties according to the official record." The letter added, "The object is to test the truth of statements that have been publicly made touching this matter, and to enable General Howard to give the facts." At this point, Howard appeared less concerned with providing individual names of victims and assailants; that came later. But even with this limited information, the military outpaced political leaders in piecing together the evidence of whether Johnson's administration protected loyalists in the South. More to the point, this start on collecting intelligence enabled Howard to move rapidly whenever Congress asked for further definitive details on the nature of law and order in the South.[43]

That situation came in January 1867 as the Senate sent to the president a resolution asking for a report on the enforcement of the Civil Rights Act. Senators wanted to know the nature of violations and, especially, steps taken to punish offenders. Many of them already knew the answer and likely expected to catch the president in a misstatement.[44] In his response to the Senate, Johnson said that he was unaware of such cases, but he had asked the heads of the executive departments for their opinions.[45] Not surprisingly, they said all was well—everyone except for the secretary of war, who, during what became an intense cabinet meeting in February, casually dropped a bomb.

Stanton had information that contradicted Johnson's impressions: a report from Howard and Grant that detailed more than 400 instances of violence. Though saying that he desired to act with the president, the secretary supported the dissemination of information that seemed to him accurate and proper (even though it contradicted Johnson's position). Then he added more ominously that if others wished to suppress the information, they certainly could try, "but there was little doubt that Members of Congress had seen this,— likely had copies."[46] To use a more contemporary phrase, the report had been leaked.

The documentation of violence stunned a majority of Johnson's advisors, but not because they believed it. Secretary of the Navy Gideon Welles concluded that collusion existed among the Radicals in Congress and the War Department to embarrass the president by amassing false information to push the country toward extreme measures with regard to the former Confederacy. At that very moment, Congress was debating a Reconstruction bill to use the military to reorganize governments in the South and to facilitate Black suffrage. Even though the report of Grant and Howard contained hundreds of murders and outrages, Welles called the list of atrocities a collection of "newspaper gossip, rumors of negro murders, neighborhood strifes and troubles." He considered the contents of the report "vague, indefinite party scandal which General Howard and his agents had picked up in newspapers and all other ways during four weeks, under and with the assistance of the War Department." The accounting of atrocities, in his view, unfairly represented the president as a liar to the American public about the peaceful nature of the rebels.[47]

Grant left a paper trail that confirmed the collaboration between him and Howard to furnish information that exposed the policies of the president that were failing to provide for equal protection under the law. He most likely was asked by Stanton to do what came next, but it is equally plausible that he would have undertaken this task even if no one had ordered it. On January 18, 1867, Grant asked Howard to compile a list of murders and other violence enacted upon freedmen or Union men in the Southern states for the prior six months or year. He was crystal clear about the reason. "My object in this," he wrote, "is to make a report showing that the Courts in the states excluded from Congress afford no security to life or property of the classes here refered [sic] to, and to recommend that Martial Law be declared over such districts as do not afford the proper protection." He called it "my" object, meaning he owned it. Howard eagerly accepted the assignment. He did not have to start from scratch: since the prior September, he had been asking for similar information from his assistant commissioners. He promised Grant to take the cases that he had "drawn off and send them to you."[48]

It was an unusual situation, to say the least. Military officers gathered data to instigate a policy change contrary to what their commander in chief wanted. They followed their own instincts about justice and constitutional duty to work in collaboration with sympathetic Radicals. Violence—often in the form of political terrorism—raged in the South, which the president of the United States and many of his Democratic supporters denied. The administration adhered to the party line that all was well. Military officers and the Freedmen's Bureau knew that it was not.

Stanton received Grant's information on February 8. It was trotted out during a cabinet meeting on February 15. Somewhere in between these dates, Stanton most likely leaked the report to Radicals, who quickly put it to use. By February 19, Senator Wilson offered a report on atrocities in the South to his colleagues on the Senate floor. Whether guilty of insubordination or deserving praise for service to their country and the cause of human rights, the military men involved saw it as a necessary action to have any chance to stop the atrocities committed in the South.

2

BLACK LIVES
IN THE RECORD

The newest acting assistant commissioner of the subdistrict of
Greenville, South Carolina, began his tour of duty by groggily fum-
bling his way to the door. It was six in the morning. A timid but persistent rapping had awakened him. A partially dressed John William
De Forest, a major with the Freedmen's Bureau, pulled the door ajar
and looked upon an African American man who begged to see the
major right away. The man's insistence convinced De Forest, allowing
him to enter as the major finished dressing in the stranger's presence. The Black man introduced himself as Cato Allums and wondered whether the name was familiar to De Forest. Allums had filed
a complaint with De Forest's predecessor because men the prior year
had robbed him. But that was old news. Allums had come because
he feared he had killed one of the white men who had just tried to
murder him.[1]

Allums reported that the encounter had begun with a knock on
his door in the dead of night. The Black man had been on guard
because he had experienced trouble before with a group of white
men nearby. Fortunately, he owned a pistol given to him by a Freedmen's Bureau officer. After Allums refused to open the door, the
intruders rammed it open with a log. Fleeing for his life, he bolted
past them through the opening as one assailant fired and missed.

As another took aim, Allums reported, "I shot him." He ran as the intruders continued firing, a bullet ripping into a fence as he vaulted it and escaped into woods. Allums's assailant later died from the wound, but Allums avoided hanging when the other assailants failed to show at a hearing. The court released the freedman, who then disappeared from the public record.[2]

The political situation also may have influenced the outcome. Former Confederates in this community knew that Northerners tried to gather damaging information on Southern violence and that their behavior in criminal matters sent messages about the safety of freedpeople. During his investigation, De Forest spoke with a local magistrate who mentioned that Northern people doubted "whether you can give a Negro a white man's chance." He convinced the major to allow civil proceedings to move forward rather than take military action. An acquittal would indicate that white people conducted justice fairly for African Americans, thus supporting the conservatives who contended that no persecution occurred. Even in this remote corner of the South, tucked in the upcountry near the Appalachian foothills, the participants understood the impact of their actions in shaping Northern impressions of Southern law and order.[3]

Other parts of De Forest's recollections, however, call into question his commitment to Black justice and demonstrate the limitations of collecting data on outrages. De Forest encountered Allums shortly after Commissioner O. O. Howard, through his circular of September 24, 1866, had ordered the tracking of murders. Every month, the major was to submit a list of outrages by Black people against whites and vice versa. His notation on Allums gave only the skimpiest details: names, date, and location—hardly energetic and certainly not something Radicals could exploit. Throughout his tenure spanning more than a year, De Forest recorded a total of only six outrages; whether this sum was the result of administering a peaceful area containing fewer Black people or due to a lack of diligence is hard to tell. At times he treated the complaints of freedmen skeptically. He once refused to provide military intervention for a Black man who claimed that two white men had threatened his life. When he learned that no shots had been fired, De Forest—without investigating further—dismissed the matter as nothing more than a "rough frolic." He sent the uneasy man away and said he heard nothing more about it. This incident did not receive mention in his monthly accounting of outrages.[4]

These examples capture the ambiguity that has made it difficult to establish a definitive assessment of the relationship between freed-people and Freedmen's Bureau agents, especially as it affected report-ing of crimes.[5] Agents often provided the only avenue for Black people seeking redress for injustice. Sometimes they found men who took their complaints to heart; other times they received less sympathy. De Forest displayed both tendencies. Even in his helpful stance with Allums, he filed a report for Washington that was rather empty and understated. And his other retelling of an outrage received no official tallying at all. Consequently, the criticism of detractors at the time, embraced even by some historians, fails to substantiate the claim that these agents always stressed rather than minimized white violence or that their bias caused a majority of them to serve as an arm of Radical Republicans and accept any report from Black people at face value.[6]

Most agents did the best they could under difficult circum-stances; however, the limitations of the Freedmen's Bureau's infra-structure, lack of clear policies, and other structural matters within the agency guaranteed that their monthly reports, contrary to Dem-ocrats' claims, understated the crimes in their jurisdictions. Southern whites also had a hand in limiting a fuller accounting of atrocities against Black people. White people used various forms of coercion to prevent African Americans from seeking justice with military author-ities, including murder.[7] Because of this, officers of the Freedmen's Bureau believed that atrocities were underreported by at least half. Meanwhile, the half that the agents gathered told a shameful story of law enforcement officers in the South turning a blind eye to, and even encouraging, slayings, beatings, burglaries, and sexual assaults.

Documentation of atrocities by the Freedmen's Bureau faced numer-ous challenges. Because the bureau was so new, its leaders often fash-ioned procedures on the fly. Keeping track of outrages evolved over time only as authorities saw the need to show what was happening in the South. Irregularities in reporting were natural in such an environment, although not in the way that Democrats claimed. It was impossible to capture a complete measure of the lawlessness in communities, with organizational, logistical, and other difficulties ensuring that the bureau underreported the nature of crime.

Although Commissioner Howard asked for an accounting of murders in September 1866, his orders stipulated no particular format. Howard at the time wasn't even interested in recording the names of the victims. Without a template, some officers supplied information in tabulated form (more quantitative), others in paragraph descriptions (more qualitative). The information represented by a particular officer also could be inconsistent. The more scrupulous officers provided names of victims and attackers, as well as the motivations for assaults. Major De Forest did not go that far in his record of the attack on Allums, omitting details entirely. He was not alone. The murders and outrages record often contained incident reports with paltry information—no names of victims, only a hazy notion of perpetrators, and no idea of the resolution of the case.

Officers did not always omit these facts, either on purpose or through negligence. Some of the reporting lay beyond their control. The information itself could be scanty, communicated by relatives or friends who did not have complete knowledge of what happened. Stories sometimes came in weeks after the original assault, preventing officers from cornering suspects who fled or from finding witnesses who could confirm the allegations. Hearsay was inevitable.

Personnel problems added another challenge for consistently gathering information. In general, the Freedmen's Bureau was short-staffed. On paper, each state had an assistant commissioner to supervise a bevy of subordinates, such as a medical officer, a finance officer, an inspector, district superintendents, an overseer of schools, and local agents hired from the communities. Also important were sub-assistant commissioners, like De Forest, who had jurisdiction over particular regions of the state, often a combination of counties.

It was rare to have all positions filled. An early history of the bureau tracked an incredible amount of turnover, beginning with the assistant commissioners. In three and a half years, fifty-four different assistant commissioners served in sixteen states and the District of Columbia. The turnover at the lower level proved even more dramatic. And the officers shouldered a crushing load of paperwork, which prevented them from maintaining a consistent and thorough tabulation of outrages. One declared, "My letters to magistrates concerning freedmen's complaints were so numerous that I only recorded the most important, leaving the vulgar herd of insignificant injuries to the uncertain labyrinths of my memory." This officer frankly admitted that he did not record all evidence of outrages because of his heavy workload.[8]

The desperation to fill positions sometimes caused officials to draw on former Confederates as subcontracted agents to provide the first point of contact for Black people for filing complaints. Without enough staff, officers had to beg for volunteers from local authorities, who absorbed the cost. Congress in the first year of the bureau's existence had appropriated no funds for salaries, forcing Freedmen's Bureau administrators to rely on people from the community to serve as agents. In Georgia, Brig. Gen. Davis Tillson petitioned the governor to authorize county officers to serve in this capacity. The governor approved, which placed former Confederates in the position of overseeing the interests of freedpeople.[9]

This did not sit well. One military officer in November 1866 complained to Tillson, "The appointment of rebels as agents of the Bureau is a foul and wicked injustice to the Freedmen, & a disgrace to the Government." He added, "The Bureau in Georgia is practically under rebel rule, and managed exclusively for the benefit of the Black man's oppressors. The law requiring employees of the Bureau to take an oath equivalent to the test-oath is not executed. The chief clerk of the Assistant Commissioner, is a rebel who served through the War, under [Confederate general] Wade Hampton."[10] African Americans likely approached such men cautiously.

Even if they were die-hard Yankees, bureau staff may not have shared an incentive to safeguard the freedpeople's welfare. The bureau was under the War Department—an extension of the military, staffed primarily by army personnel. Army protocols gave officers of the Freedmen's Bureau little choice in the soldiers who fell under their command. They were assigned, not selected. When author John T. Trowbridge toured the South, he met an officer in Memphis who complained that the law establishing the bureau did not permit him to choose his own soldiers for duty. Some of the detailed soldiers, he said, "were always incompetent, or neglectful of their duties, or so prejudiced for or against the Blacks that they were incapable of administering justice." A few, he said, remained in sympathy with slavery. Others were seduced by the planters or local Democrats who massaged their egos or showered them with social favors.[11] Undoubtedly many of these detailed men hoped to be mustered out of the service and sent home rather than saddled with the tedium of record keeping.

The more problematic agents populated the lower ranks, such as the civilian men recruited from communities; officers at the top underwent stronger vetting and generally had intentions to help the transition of the formerly enslaved to freedom. This does not mean, though, they were perfectly sympathetic to the predicaments of African Americans. Only one of the assistant commissioners chosen originally by Howard could be considered a full-fledged abolitionist. Most had been generals who served with Howard or had come to the attention of the secretary of war. They were primarily native-born, college educated, and from the North. Howard himself was known for his strong Christianity, and he liked men of similar stock. But whether or not they met his own religious standards, he tended to seek conscientious men. As a group, unlike what critics maintained, they hardly could be considered uniformly Radical. Yet these assistant commissioners were not blind to the inequities that African Americans faced. Most of them did not believe in the equality of the races, but when it came to justice for freedpeople, they held strongly to the principle of equality before the law.[12]

Beyond personnel matters, the quick establishment of a bureau, without organizational precedents or consistent guidelines, to handle the lives of millions of people ensured that even men with the best intentions faced enormous problems. Two military officers enlisted by President Johnson to inspect the bureau—Generals

James B. Steedman and J. S. Fullerton—underscored the disordered nature of an agency patched together to handle radical upheaval in social, economic, and political relations. But the report they produced was a biased one; Johnson intended to prove that Congress should disband the bureau and had selected men who agreed with him for an inspection. Reading against the grain of the conclusions nonetheless underscores the procedural problems that beset the agency, especially when it came to the oversight of criminal behavior.

Steedman and Fullerton noted that the bureau had no "settled mode of administration" and little uniformity in procedures. Officers applied different policies as they adapted to the peculiar circumstances within their jurisdiction. In one state, officers exerted judicial powers; in another, they turned over cases to civil authorities; in still another, they turned conflicts over to provost courts, which were military bodies. In some areas, officers tried to regulate wages; in other places, they did not. In some states, the bureau interceded on behalf of freedpeople; in others, its officers coerced the freedmen to the advantage of planters.[13]

The report added to the impression that violence in the South had been overblown. First, Steedman and Fullerton admitted that antagonism and bloodshed did exist in one place: "There is still more ill feeling existing between the whites and blacks in Mississippi than elsewhere." So-called organized desperadoes held the town of Grenada in terror, and snipers had fired at night at the mayor in Meridian. But they challenged an officer in Columbus who had estimated that two-thirds of the planters in his neighborhood had committed outrages on freedpeople. "On investigation," they noted, "we found the statements of this officer as to the ill treatment of negroes grossly exaggerated, and learned that the agent himself had, on one occasion, advised a planter with whom he was dining to 'club' any negro who refused to work." The generals concluded that aside from certain areas of Mississippi, freedpeople received kind treatment from whites. They rationalized that capitalist principles smoothed over race relations: that the labor value of Black people in the marketplace furnished them protection.[14]

But it did not, especially if freedpeople risked trying to report their side of the story to local agents of the bureau. Time and again employers or local thugs intimidated or gunned down Black men and women on their way to air their grievances before military officers.[15]

Despite these issues that undoubtedly restrained reports of violence, most bureau officials did their best—given their own limitations—to account for the atrocities in their jurisdictions. And Black people, although aware of the dangers they faced and the problematic nature of the military personnel, still tried to tell their stories, even though the vast majority of complaints received little satisfaction. For Black people, justice in early Reconstruction remained an aspiration, not a reality. African Americans could not testify in courts or sit on juries until after Radical Reconstruction began in 1867. For the most part, the criminal justice system typically punished rather than protected them. Military justice provided one of the few avenues of possible retribution, despite imperfections. And even if no justice came, it was worth placing a violation of human rights on record in a government document. The act of reporting itself, according to one historian, provided a means of resistance for freedpeople.[16]

And so freedpeople went in droves to military officers, just as Cato Allums did when he appeared on the doorstep of John William De Forest. They came for many purposes, including to complain about the need for schools, about planters who refused to pay wages, about families torn asunder as white people enforced apprenticeship laws, and about many more circumstances. They also came because of the outrages committed against them, their relatives, and their neighbors. In 1868, one report to Congress noted of North Carolina, "The offices of the bureau were thronged day after day from dawn till dark by the victims of these wrongs, many of them having travelled on foot several days to find a friend who would defend and protect them." The assistant commissioner of the state noted that his personnel had adjudicated 3,405 such cases within one quarter of the year. Thomas D. Eliot, Republican congressman from Massachusetts who served as chair of the Committee on Freedmen's Affairs, extrapolated from the figure that more than 100,000 complaints may have been heard by bureau officers in a single year across the

South. Whether the estimate was accurate, little doubt existed that freedpeople sought intervention by the military to fight against the numerous transgressions that they faced within a civil system that practiced unequal justice.[17]

Although the problems in record keeping gave critics ammunition to argue that the material was tainted and thus worthless, reports from the bureau represented hard-won evidence that accurately portrayed the larger patterns of violence within Southern communities. But Democrats refused to believe what became increasingly damning testimony of the white South's rejection of the terms of reunion.

Over the course of three-plus years, officers collected and identified 3,981 incident reports under the title of "Records Relating to Murders and Outrages" (table 2.1). The material has been preserved by the National Archives on microfilm involving eight states of the former Confederacy and the District of Columbia. Although most of the incidents span 1866 through the end of 1868, when the Freedmen's Bureau began a phased reduction in personnel, the record includes some crimes reported during 1865. The record overall contains the fate of between 5,000 and 6,000 people, since one incident report could include multiple victims. In other words, an account might contain one killed, another wounded, and a third who escaped. Counted as one report, the item actually contained a murder, a physical assault, and an attempted slaying.

With the exception of Louisiana, physical assaults tended to be more numerous than murders. We gathered under physical assaults a wide variety of incidents, such as knifings, whippings, burnings, beatings, or other kinds of physical contact that harmed the individual but fell short of death. Some involved quite minor encounters, while other serious attacks left victims incapacitated. Verbal assaults featured abusive comments but more often threats of murder or other punitive measures if the person did not change a particular behavior or tried to report atrocities to Union officials. This is the kind of encounter that De Forest had dismissed as a "rough frolic."

TABLE 2.1. TYPES OF MURDERS AND OUTRAGES BY STATE, 1865–1868

Type	AL	GA	LA	NC	SC	TN	TX	VA	DC	Total
Incident reports	69	451	507	192	146	65	2,288	162	101	3,981
Murders	18	160	529	9	19	21	859	19	0	1,634
Physical assaults	35	306	480	153	92	30	1,259	95	38	2,488
Verbal assaults	3	15	25	17	8	8	120	8	14	218
Sexual assaults	1	1	9	6	0	2	15	3	0	37
Theft/damage	3	3	41	15	14	10	101	19	5	211
Political intent	0	27	35	0	14	0	28	5	4	113
Civil court	1	48	46	26	25	7	226	13	0	392
Military court	0	10	6	8	8	5	15	0	0	52
Convictions	0	4	4	23	7	5	46	7	0	96
Fines levied	0	2	3	8	1	2	254	6	0	276
Unspecified	66					35				101

Sources: Alabama (reel 23, M809), Georgia (reel 32, M798), Louisiana (reel 34, M1027), North Carolina (reel 33, M84), South Carolina (reel 34, M869), Tennessee (reel 34, M999), Texas (reel 32, M821), Virginia (reel 59, M1048), Washington (reel 21, M1055), all in RG 105, BRFAL, NA.

In looking at the regions of greatest violence, the Lower South stands out, particularly the states of Georgia, Louisiana, and Texas. The Lone Star State, in fact, led the way with a mind-boggling 2,288 incident reports of atrocities—nearly 60 percent of all outrages. Murders there exceeded 800, and various kinds of physical assaults numbered 1,259. The number of whites killed outnumbered Blacks over a three-year period, although narrowly. Most of the white deaths involved "Union men," indicating those who had either opposed secession, failed to back the Confederacy, or hailed from the North. Former Confederates might assassinate anyone who stood in the way of their securing local power. White supremacists often claimed they used violence to fend off a "race war"—meaning alleged agitation by Black people and their Unionist comrades—but the numbers fail to support this assertion. White people were by far the main instigators of violence.[18]

Louisiana totaled 507 incident reports of murders and outrages, followed by Georgia with 451. Power struggles repeatedly tore apart the Pelican State, which resulted in more than 500 homicides. Based on work done on the state by other scholars, that figure was certainly underreported. The early occupation of New Orleans in 1862 made it a center of political conflict over Reconstruction, and a well-known massacre took place there in July 1866. Federal officials paired the state with Texas for administrative purposes, placing both under the command of Maj. Gen. Philip Sheridan—a no-nonsense subordinate of Gen. Ulysses S. Grant's who relished tough stands against former Confederates. Georgia also was a troublesome state, featuring political assassinations. Commissioner Howard at one point erupted in a letter, "Is it really so, that no man can say what he thinks in Augusta, Ga. without being in danger of offending the delicate sensibilities of the enemies of the country! Must we bow and scrape forever?"[19]

Tennessee represented a special case that resulted in an underreporting of violence. The state, which seems to have come in last in number of complaints, actually had a notorious track record, causing Maj. Gen. George Thomas to beg for troops to help quell terrorism by the Ku Klux Klan. Because Tennessee had been considered reconstructed early, it escaped the initial cataloging of atrocities. The record for the state was assembled rather quickly, with cases scraped together from 1865 and into 1866. Klan violence became an increasing factor in 1868 and caused a congressional inquiry to request special data from the Freedmen's Bureau then, which made it into a government report, but one whose findings have remained separate from the main record. The congressional numbers of Klan activity, when added to the record of murders and outrages cited in table 2.1, meant the state ran neck and neck with Georgia for homicides.[20]

The rest of the states fell considerably lower in notations of violence, although this does not suggest a peaceful accommodation to racial adjustment. Most likely there are other peculiarities in the data collection that account for the anomalies. And timing was everything when it came to tracking outbreaks of violence. Flare-ups occurred idiosyncratically based on local political struggles. North Carolina, which looks more peaceful in table 2.1, became a center of concern over the Ku Klux Klan during hearings in the early 1870s, and South Carolina produced its own record of terrorism that increased after the bureau quit tracking violence. Virginia contained former Whigs who avoided the imposition of Radical Reconstruction by agreeing to Black suffrage so that white leaders maintained home rule. They hoped to project an aura of peace. Even so, they often failed to hold the underlying tensions in check. Howard stated that violence at times exploded in Virginia. "At Petersburg, they have burned their churches," he wrote in 1866. "At Hampton they are burning houses, school buildings, churches etc. We must do right firmly, and not yield too far." It is likely that not all of these crimes made it into the record of murders and outrages.[21]

Mysteriously, information from three states—Arkansas, Florida, and Mississippi—was not integrated into the reporting of the murders and outrages. No clear evidence explains why the system of record keeping and reporting by assistant commissioners failed to account for those three states; other sources certainly reveal episodes of violence there, and even the report of Steedman and Fullerton, who diminished the news of outrages, cited Mississippi as a contrary example. Those who know the vast manuscript collections of the Freedmen's Bureau understand that similar records may exist apart from the main reports. Whatever the case, it is important not to overstate geographic concentrations of white violence against freedpeople in light of this significant gap in the formal reporting.[22]

The record overall confirmed what Radical politicians preached but their opponents denied—that the legal system did not serve African Americans. As table 2.1 indicates, most of the cases involving assaults on Black people and white Unionists never went to court or experienced anything remotely resembling justice. Convictions amounted to a ridiculously low total of ninety-six across all jurisdictions over the course of three years. Clearly, no justice existed in civil law for Black people in the post-emancipation South. The negligence of local law enforcement to arrest and prosecute suspects encouraged white people to employ coercion to pin down labor, punishing the freedpeople who stepped out of line and murdering the federal officials and white Unionists who got in the way.

In the rare instances in which convictions occurred, the data do not reveal whether authorities enforced the decisions. Community attitudes could block the outcomes of the bureau. In Texas, a sub-assistant commissioner fined a citizen for threatening the life of President Johnson. The sheriff considered the fine illegal and tried to arrest the bureau officer, who had to seek sanctuary with the commander of the military post. Bowing to community pressure, superiors reassigned the sub-assistant commissioner to Austin.[23] Bureau personnel tried to protect freedpeople, but they swam against the tide of local whites, who detested these non–civil court actions as an imposition of military rule and both openly and tacitly sanctioned resistance.

At least one other regional peculiarity leaped out from the tabulation—the Washington, D.C., area demonstrated how slave owners resisted emancipation and how freedom did not allow some Black parents control over their children. White planters, who did not want to lose their power over enslaved people, used new apprenticeship laws to tear children from parents. Of the 101 incidents mentioned by the bureau for the District of Columbia (which included cases from Maryland), slightly under half of them concerned masters using the legal system to deprive African American parents of custody of their children.

After the Civil War, in the states of the former Confederacy as well as in the border states like Maryland, legal statutes gave preference to former masters for the care of children whose parents allegedly did not have the financial means to do so. White people maintained that former slaves could not transition to freedom without becoming dependent. They argued that even in freedom Black people required force to work. And they claimed it was better to remove children from parents who could not administer proper care and to place them with people who could. Invariably, this turned out to be former masters. In the apprentice process, parents of the African American children generally could not testify, nor could they prove their solvency. Black people turned to the Freedmen's Bureau to challenge these decisions and try to preserve their families.[24]

The record of murders and outrages reveals the desperation that parents exhibited in these tragic cases. Shortly after the Maryland state constitution instituted emancipation in 1864, Basil Crowdy and his wife in Calvert County had their three children taken away through a "legal" form of enslavement. The court bound the children to Mr. R. D. Sollay "despite the refusal of both parents to consent." Understandably, Mrs. Crowdy lost emotional control during the proceedings. A constable at the hearing, "finding the mother obstinate[,] and deaf to reason, struck her in the face with his fist in the presence of the Judges." The sting of that blow and the frustration over losing her children to a white master endured. Although the incident happened in December 1864, the Freedmen's Bureau recorded the incident on June 16, 1866. Eighteen months had not blunted the anguish of these parents who kept trying to reclaim their children. Unfortunately, the documents remain silent about whether they succeeded.[25]

They were by no means alone in their struggles, but that fact provided no comfort for them or for the others caught in this awful law. Maryland featured numerous instances of former masters attempting to pin down labor by apprenticing Black children, many of them former slaves. As soon as the laws allowed in late 1864, about 1,000 freed children had been seized in two Maryland counties alone. By the fall of 1866, officials reported an additional 1,200 indentures. In the Eastern Shore counties, some 1,600 Black children had come under this procedure. The practice was going strong until late 1867, when Supreme Court chief justice Salmon P. Chase, while riding circuit, ruled against these apprenticeship relations as a violation of the Civil Rights Act and the Thirteenth Amendment.[26]

These accounts in the Washington area contain their own mystery of how they became part of the record of murders and outrages. The incidents occurred before Commissioner Howard directed his subordinates to trace the lawlessness in the South. That these early cases from the Washington area ended up with the other murders and outrages material suggested that Howard dipped into older reports to gather the information for lawmakers and others who might help press for the elimination of this atrocity. We know the practice of separating children from parents distressed him. He made a point of commenting on this particular outrage in his annual report for 1867: a primary goal of the Freedmen's Bureau had been to unite

TABLE 2.2. VICTIMS AND ASSAILANTS, 1865–1868

Type	AL	GA	LA	NC	SC	TN	TX	VA	DC	Total
• Victims										
Women	22	62	61	48	36	13	288	22	26	578
Ministers	2	2	4	0	2	2	1	2	6	21
Freedmen's Bureau agents/soldiers	2	6	4	2	1	1	51	2	2	71
Black veterans	1	0	0	1	1	1	8	1	6	19
• Assailants										
Two or more	11	67	119	26	33	18	274	11	12	571
Ku Klux Klan	0	4	12	0	6	7	10	9	0	48

Sources: Alabama (reel 23, M809), Georgia (reel 32, M798), Louisiana (reel 34, M1027), North Carolina (reel 33, M84), South Carolina (reel 34, M869), Tennessee (reel 34, M999), Texas (reel 32, M821), Virginia (reel 59, M1048), Washington (reel 21, M1055), all in RG 105, BRFAL, NA.

families, not to separate them.[27] The reporting represented yet one more circumstance in which Howard used data to expose an injustice to freedpeople. The struggles over apprenticeship served as only one form of coercion imposed on newly freed Black women, with former masters using both the law and violence to redraw racial and sexual borders. Black women stood out for the frequency of their appearance in the record of murders and outrages. Table 2.2 shows the people, both victims and assailants, identified by bureau officials as being involved in the conflicts. Women, ministers, community leaders, and soldiers all faced violence that caught the attention of federal authorities. Black women, however, constituted the largest of these subgroups. Although women represented only roughly 15 percent of the total incident reports, in a number of states the attacks on them ranged from one-fifth to one-third: Alabama at 32 percent; North and South Carolina, 25 percent; and Tennessee, 20 percent. And if we consider the complaints from people who lost custody of children to apprentice laws, the presence of women in the reporting only increases. As always in the case of gender conflicts, the incidents that became part of a government record most likely made up only a fraction of the real numbers.

The appearance of Black women in the record is noteworthy. The fact that they testified at all about the criminal behavior of whites to a government entity represented an enormous change from antebellum days. Before the war, free Blacks typically could not testify against white people before local, state, or federal judges. During the war, Union military commissions led a change in this status quo as they prosecuted rape charges by Black women against soldiers. Newly freed Black women gained the right to legally testify as victims of sexual assault in military courts, as well as to contest other crimes. In a study of Missouri, one scholar also captured how military commissions heard instances of crimes against formerly enslaved women during the war, showing their persistence and creativity in transforming civil and domestic concerns into military affairs. After emancipation but before new state constitutions clarified the right of Black testimony in civil courts, the Freedmen's Bureau provided another avenue for women to pursue claims of justice when they may have had nowhere else to go.[28]

And the officers, on balance, took the women's accounts seriously—something that Democrats and conservatives in the North or South refused to do. Long-standing traditions of criminal justice built on racism and gender discrimination fortified the critics who refused to consider the testimony of African Americans as credible.

The example of Major De Forest, though, cautions that even helpful officers sometimes showed little enthusiasm for investigating crimes, which may have contributed to underreporting criminal behavior against women. This seems to have been the case with rapes, which represented the least reported outrage against women. Such a lack does not contradict historians' accounts of white men frequently raping Black women, though. Most likely, the diminished presence in these particular reports reflected the difficulty of traversing geographic distance to file reports (most freedpeople lived in rural areas away from Freedmen's Bureau officers stationed in towns), the prejudice of men in general against accepting Black women's reporting of sexual assault, the intimidation by white men against women reporting the crimes, and the trauma that can dissuade a woman from exposing herself to a prejudiced criminal justice system.[29]

Gender norms, however, afforded Black women no special protection from sexual assaults. One study revealed at least two instances of gang rape, one of them during the Memphis massacre of 1866. The murder and outrages record contained others, such as when John Washington and John Graham "ravished" Susan Gooseley, a Black woman, hanging her up by the thumbs and striking her over the head with a pistol. She had to flee her home in Davis County, Texas, to save her life.[30]

The bureau reporting also showed Black women fighting for control of their bodies and defending their right to children born of interracial relations with former masters. Conflicts came over resolving mixed-race relations that existed before the war, many of them the product of coercion. Historians have estimated the number of mulattoes in the South at between 10 and 12 percent in 1860, although the people of mixed-race unions made up more significant proportions of city dwellers: 39 percent of free Blacks and 20 percent of the enslaved. These numbers came from a society that publicly frowned upon amalgamation of the races. Given the supposed stigma against such associations—and the possible embarrassment when encountering a census marshal—more mixed-race offspring existed than appeared in the government records.[31]

Several incidents in the record exposed these conflicts between white men and Black women regarding who took custody of a mixed-race child or who held the power to determine sexual partners. In Tennessee, a white man named James Riley attacked a former slave, Catherine Riley, and kidnapped her child. He resisted giving up the child when a public official ordered the youngster returned to the mother. Riley rode to the mother's location, beat her with a club until she was senseless, and took the child, stating that he hoped to "put it out of reach of the d—d Yankees." In South Carolina, Albert Hamlin spirited the son of Winnie Anderson to Alabama, keeping the boy out of reach of the mother. The record did not state if the mother saw her son again. And in Georgia, Nelson Ladford beat and shot at Harriett Blackwell, who had come to declare that he had fathered her child. Community sentiments may have been on her side as authorities, in a rare display, arrested Ladford and bound him over to local court.[32] Finally, one complaint revealed that a child held by a former master turned out to be six and a half years old, not eighteen as the man alleged. A person of that age could hardly have been essential for the laboring needs of a farm. It seems likely that the perpetrator tried to keep one of the children he had fathered with a woman under slavery.[33]

These conflicts likely arose from a number of motivations: spite of the white men, a desire to control a woman's sexual relations by preying on her motherly instincts, the intention to keep a child fathered illegitimately during slavery. Whatever the underlying causes of these outrages, the record reveals yet one more wrenching side of the transition to freedom in which the undoing and remaking of family relations took a particular toll on freedwomen. Rarely did such situations reflect themselves in debates in Congress or the public press. They more often were overlooked.

Then there are the more clear-cut, although no less repugnant, cases when men tried to force sexual concessions, failed, and meted out horrible consequences. In March 1868, John Cautly killed a woman in Texas because she would not commit adultery with him. Tilman Curboo did the same to Virginia Harrison, who "would not yield to his desires."[34] More complicated was the case of D. Beasley, who had cohabited for seventeen years with a woman identified as Minerva. After abandoning the home for more than a year, he returned, only to be spurned by Minerva in his sexual advances. In response, he drove out both Minerva and seventy-year-old Unity, who had nursed him as a child. The Freedmen's Bureau ordered him to take back the victims or face imprisonment, but nothing indicated how the matter resolved.[35]

The existence of Black women's testimony in the record showed they embraced a sense of citizenship and loyalty to the nation that made them determined to fight for equality under the law. They turned the Freedmen's Bureau, as one historian observed, into an ally in the battle to define freedom. In risking their lives to supply information on atrocities to bureau agents, they asserted the right to live free of violence and to maintain the ability to control their bodies. Freedwomen in these new circumstances represented a political threat, even without voting rights, as they made public legal issues out of supposedly private domestic conflicts. Households served as sites of power struggles involving new racial and sexual relations. Additionally, Black women took on identities as Unionists and sided with both Black and white men in political fights. And they involved themselves in the struggles with their men to resist violence intended to construct white supremacy.[36]

One report revealed women's struggles in the political arena to eliminate segregation on public transportation. Black women in the North employed tactics similar to those of Rosa Parks in the modern civil rights movement by riding in the white section of cars, forcing an arrest, and then using the incident to file suit. On February 1, 1868, a similar incident happened near Gordonsville, Virginia. A Freedmen's Bureau officer reported the conductor of the railroad between Richmond and Fredericksburg had "put out" three Black women because of their race, meaning he evicted them from the train. He noted that the women wished to file suit in the U.S. District Court to take advantage of the Civil Rights Act. The bureau officer noted that the legal papers had been filed and forwarded to a U.S. District Attorney, but no outcome was reported.[37] Here again women immediately seized upon legal mechanisms, testifying to their sense of rights as citizens in enjoying the ability to bring complaints to the government.

Violence came to women, just as it did to men who demonstrated signs of independence or, especially, political mobilization. Freedpeople understood that the atrocities originated from more than emotion—they also revealed a tactical mindset that increasingly expressed itself as a nascent insurgency against the upheaval in power in the post-emancipation South.

President Johnson and his Democrat supporters based their arguments for Reconstruction policies on the impression that former rebels accepted their fate, recognized federal authority, and conducted peaceful relations with freedpeople. They rejected any evidence that countered a position that favored quick reunion with political rights restored to former Confederates. Yet they could not have been more wrong.

Military personnel in the South knew that individual acts of violence hinted at a more organized power struggle. Occasionally, Freedmen's Bureau officers fielded complaints of bands of men acting in concert as self-described "regulators," which echoed resistance to taxes and fees by colonial officials. The soldiers encountering the violence called them desperadoes, bushwhackers, and bandits. The bands of men operated with impunity, with the tacit and open sanction of community leaders, law enforcement officers, magistrates, and judges. It took the U.S. Army until later in the century to come up with a name for these low-intensity conflicts to effect political change: insurgencies.[38]

Insurgencies are fought not only with guns but also with the complicity of political and legal officials. According to a contemporary State Department report, it is "the organized use of subversion and violence to seize, nullify or challenge political control of a region. As such, it is primarily a political struggle, in which both sides use armed force to create space for their political, economic and influence activities to be effective." People do not necessarily wage an insurgency as a single group with a centralized, military-style command structure "but may involve a complex matrix of different actors with various aims, loosely connected in dynamic and non-hierarchical networks." The tools of an insurgency fall into three areas: persuasion, which uses ideology as well as money and control of land; subversion, in which people disrupt government institutions and organizations; and coercion, especially violence but also economic control and tactics aimed at government officials to dissuade them from taking measures to prevent outrages.[39]

The conquered South featured these activities even before paramilitary organizations like the Ku Klux Klan became a visible force.[40] Democratic newspapers undergirded ideological resistance and fed racial anger over alleged indignities suffered from Black resistance to white privilege. Southern employers did what they could to coerce labor. Land redistribution to formerly enslaved people was nipped in the bud. Even early in Reconstruction, we can find actions intended to achieve a political effect—to diminish federal control over race-labor relations. Collusion existed throughout the legal system to enable white violence against Black men and women as part of the shaping of a new order. Confederates could not win a conventional war against the U.S. Army, but white Southerners contained their losses through administering the offices of sheriffs, constables, judges, and other posts within the legal system. To officers of the Freedmen's Bureau, a disturbing number of assaults suggested that the violence often had more widespread intentions behind it than settling personal scores.

At first glance that evidence may not leap from the catalog of cruelties in the Records Relating to Murders and Outrages. Group activity provides one place to look for people acting in concert, yet across the records of Freedmen's Bureau personnel, only 571 (roughly 15 percent of the incident reports) specifically mentioned more than one person involved in committing an outrage. If the reports that singled out community leaders as part of the atrocities (doctors, lawyers, sheriffs, municipal officials) are added, the figure creeps up to 16 percent of the incident reports.

Although these figures fall far short of a majority, the tendency of terrorists to act in groups, no matter how infrequently, registered strongly on bureau officials. They feared that such incidents signaled a resurgence of the rebel spirit and expressed their concern when seeing bands of men acting in concert. That legal authorities failed to respond or looked the other way also troubled federal authorities. After a band of lawless men murdered nine to fifteen freedpeople in Tennessee, a bureau officer remarked, "Their numbers are so formidable that they overawe the peaceable, quiet citizens, and they have things their own way." The word "overawe" served as the euphemism for the lack of local enforcement. It was a charitable interpretation that presumed local officials even cared at all to protect freedpeople by prosecuting white men.[41]

The combination of vigilante activity with the lack of law enforcement spoke volumes to the military personnel stationed in the South. Without local courts and criminal proceedings holding perpetrators accountable, the justice system encouraged the continuation of atrocities and revealed a community-wide acceptance of violence as a tool for restructuring the social, economic, and political terrain. Bureau officers studiously noted whenever elites participated. More often, leaders in communities were satisfied to let others do the dirty work and to help cover up the circumstances through a sham of criminal justice.

Freedmen's Bureau officers experienced community resistance personally. In late 1865, unidentified residents of Fayette, Mississippi, broke into the office of the sub-commissioner of the Freedmen's Bureau, burned valuable papers, and stole revenue stamps and money. This was an assault on federal authority, yet local officials looked the other way. At roughly the same time of year, Captain Warren Peck, an officer in Copiah County, Mississippi, faced worse circumstances. Residents there seized this representative of the U.S. military, confining him for three days in an iron cage in the county jail that was only five feet high, five feet wide, and seven feet long. Although forced to sleep in the cage for an additional seven nights, Peck's captors let him out during daytime, while restricting him to the confines of the jail. The mob who "arrested" him was led by the sheriff of the county. Peck was tried by "an incompetent country Justice of the Peace." Understandably, the imprisoned Peck could not come up with the bond of $2,000 to guarantee his presence before the circuit court. It was an exorbitant sum, especially for a man constrained behind iron bars. What finally earned his release? Force by the U.S. military.[42] Collusion existed among law enforcement personnel to allow this infringement of rights.

One example captured the often-shameless nature of how public officials in the former Confederacy flaunted the legal system when it came to Black people. It was not the worst of the atrocities that one encounters in the Records Relating to Murders and Outrages, although it was bad enough for the woman suffering the ordeal. How this one instance played out, however, symbolized the agreement among law enforcement personnel to let violence against Black people go unpunished.

In Louisiana during the late summer of 1865, a white man named Damascus D. Day slashed with a knife Mary Stewart, a freedwoman.

She was contracted as a day laborer to Thomas Day—perhaps the father of Damascus—until January 1866. Discord arose over some facet of her working arrangements. When Day threatened to kill her, Stewart fled but was caught and returned to the white man's house. There, he cut her on the head with a knife while his mother begged him not to kill the freedwoman. That pleading saved Stewart's life, but it did not stop Day from slashing her twice on an arm and then stabbing her in the side. This was nothing out of the ordinary. The act was fairly typical of violent encounters between white men and Black women in the post-emancipation South. It was, however, unusual that authorities ordered Day to New Orleans for trial.

Predictably, neither Stewart nor witnesses on her behalf appeared at the appointed time. The Freedmen's Bureau officer reporting on the case supposed that intimidation had occurred. Most likely Day or his acquaintances had let Mary Stewart know the punishment that awaited if she pushed the issue forward. The next step after such a slashing would have been to finish the job through murder. Stewart took the prudent course to stay away from a tainted proceeding. But then the story took a turn that made it more than a knifing incident.[43]

Instead of being punished, Day was "immediately afterward" (in the wording of the Freedmen's Bureau officer) appointed by local authorities to serve on the grand jury that was in session. These legal entities consisted of people from the community who heard a district attorney or other officer of the court represent the facts of cases to determine whether evidence existed to issue a true bill to take the matter to trial. The grand jury did not decide on guilt or innocence, only whether enough wrongdoing occurred to warrant a hearing. As such, the grand jurors served as the gatekeepers for the community's definition of crimes.

Here was Damascus D. Day, the slasher of a woman and someone who either intimidated the witness himself or who had friends discourage her from testifying, rewarded with a position of authority in which he helped determine whether complaints had sufficient evidence to move forward with prosecution. The speed with which this occurred—"immediately afterward"—made an impression on the officer recording this affair. It was a slap in the face for African Americans and white Republicans for the sheer hubris conveyed by the court's appointment of a man guilty of assault with intent to murder to serve as one of the arbiters of crime.[44]

It requires little energy to find in bureau reports more instances of civil authorities contradicting the statements of President Johnson and Democrats that magistrates in the South performed their jobs without racial bias. The assistant superintendent of the bureau at Suffolk, Virginia, reported in June 1866 that outrages occurred there frequently. One in particular captured his attention for the signal it sent that public officials fought, rather than aided, the efforts to preserve law and order. A party of white ruffians had walked down the streets of Suffolk assaulting every Black person in sight. White citizens took no notice. Later in the day, the men nearly killed two older Black men with bricks. The assistant superintendent sought help from the mayor, who passed the buck by telling the officer that it was the chief magistrate who handled these matters. As expected, the magistrate refused to act and, instead, dumped the situation back into the mayor's hands. Meanwhile, enough time had passed during these bureaucratic arguments to allow the ruffians to ride away.

Undaunted, the Freedmen's Bureau officer exercised his own authority to arrest the ringleader. Because he could not adjudicate the crime himself, the officer handed the man over to the deputy sheriff. Within ten minutes, the sheriff let the accused man walk. So ended this particular episode, but not the longer-term struggles.[45]

Even though justice rarely came, it mattered that the military stationed in the South provided evidence of violence that many Northerners still refused to believe. It was important to have hard facts about how civil authorities condoned outrages against Black people and white representatives of the government. Information supplied by the bureau added to the rationale for military intervention in civil affairs, especially to show that republican governments did not exist and that there was not equal protection before the law. Hard-core Radicals justified federal intervention by saying the South existed as conquered provinces or that the North held the South in a grasp of war.[46] Moderate Republicans needed more coaxing. The violence documented in the Records Relating to Murders and Outrages would help to make the case.

3

AND THE
MILITARY COMES

Democrats in February 1867 mounted a vigorous defense during debates over whether to enact martial law in the South. They dismissed Radical claims of lawlessness as propaganda to expand political power through military interference in civilian affairs. They also claimed that their own informants disputed the compilation of atrocities in what they demeaned as Senator Henry Wilson's "little book."[1] Democrats further attacked Radicals for withholding names of letter-writers in accounts they claimed unfairly impugned white Southerners. They alleged that even Wilson's table of cases, despite listing identities and sources, told a biased story with adulterated evidence. Some belittled the officers of the Freedmen's Bureau for incompetence in records administration and for creating lies so they could seize Southern plantations. Garrett Davis of Kentucky typified many opponents of military intervention when he said, "I believe that in the State of New York there are more outrages and crimes of that character than in any half dozen Southern States." In other words, violence in the South reflected only what existed in American society writ large.[2]

Republicans disagreed. They believed that white loyalists and freedpeople faced lawlessness from a former enemy who refused to accept the results of the war. The violence by ex-Confederates had overwhelmed law enforcement as rebels used undemocratic means to try to regain control of their region. Only the army could solve this problem. Yet Republicans had to show that conditions were as bad as they represented. They needed information that countered the inevitable denial of President Johnson and the Democrats in a partisan climate in order to validate as constitutional a rare application of military power in a democracy.

The rationale for intervention differed. Radical Republicans like Thaddeus Stevens of Pennsylvania argued that Congress could impose any measures it wished on the South because it was conquered territory; others saw the Confederacy as still on a wartime footing and thus open to reunification as the victors saw fit. Moderate Republicans, though, supported military administration because Black and white loyalists had little protection of their life, liberty, or property. These Republican legislators invoked article IV, section 4, of the Constitution empowering Congress to "guarantee to every State in this Union a Republican Form of Government." Republicans interpreted this "guarantee clause" to mean that a republic based on representative government must ensure that citizens received equal protection under the law.[3]

To gather more information on Southern behavior, Republicans in Congress conducted various fact-finding missions, including sending representatives into parts of the former Confederacy. Meanwhile, they engaged the Freedmen's Bureau to provide Congress with details about murders and outrages in the South. The results, exemplified in the documentation by Henry Wilson, changed the way information was presented. And the situation turned the Freedmen's Bureau, an agency of the executive branch, into a de facto investigatory arm of the legislative branch—a role that continued throughout the bureau's remaining time in the South. Meanwhile, as the army took over governance of the former Confederacy after passage of the Military Reconstruction Act in March 1867, Freedmen's Bureau agents helped to qualify voters, enabling Black men to cast ballots while disqualifying white men considered disloyal. This created a backlash by Southern and Northern Democrats who raised renewed protests that falsely accused the Radicals of exaggerating the violence to rationalize the imposition of military power over the South.

⸻

In December 1866, Republicans sent more than forty representatives from both houses of Congress on a tour through Memphis and down to New Orleans. Three members of the Select Committee on the New Orleans massacre of 1866 had convened hearings in the Crescent City. The larger group of congressmen, some accompanied by wives, took advantage of the holiday adjournment to see how matters progressed and to check the pulse of Southerners in general. It turned into an excursion similar to General Grant's tour a year earlier, as they ate and drank with former Confederate military officers, particularly Gen. P. G. T. Beauregard. Northern commentators took heart that good feelings prevailed and that civil behavior greeted the travelers. The *Crisis*, a Democratic newspaper in Ohio, hoped that the "dead-head excursion" convinced the sightseers that they had misrepresented the South "most outrageously"[4]

Other Democrats feared the tour would only intensify the storm. The *New York World*, a leading Democratic newspaper in New York City, considered the "flying trip" a superficial one. Even though it stood to enlighten the participants a little, they would encounter men who had "hearts full of gall" because they only wanted to court the favor of Northern agitators, referring to white Unionists who also faced persecution from former rebels. "In every community there are men born to be croakers," the reporter stated, adding that he expected men of this stamp to seek out the excursionists. "Of course, no true knowledge of the temper and disposition of the Southern people is to be gathered from such sources." The need for such a trip proved to this writer that the legislators had no understanding of the South. "It is scandalous," he added, "that the meagre information hurriedly caught up by these roving Republicans, should comprise the whole stock of local Southern knowledge possessed by a body whose main business . . . is to legislate on Southern questions." The solution? Admit the Southern representatives who remained unseated by Congress. Only these men—some of them former Confederate military and political figures—had direct knowledge of the Southern condition.[5]

Congressional attempts to acquire information bore fruit in time for the debate over using the army to manage political change in the South. Several pieces of supporting information returned to Congress in early 1867: the report of the July 1866 New Orleans massacre, the slayings of three Union soldiers in South Carolina, and the more extensive cataloging of murders and outrages by the Freedmen's Bureau. All portrayed a South where Black and white loyalists faced little protection by law enforcement. In fact, the police represented part of the problem.

The report on the massacre involved testimony from more than seventy people during hearings held in both Washington and New Orleans. Violence had exploded as white and Black men tried to revive the constitutional convention of 1864 to eliminate the Black Codes that resembled slavery. The confrontation by conservative whites intended to decide the struggle for political power in their favor. The conservative mayor mobilized his police force to break up the convention, with killings occurring outside the Mechanics Institute and again as officers forced their way into the hall to shoot participants at point-blank range. The report told of African Americans slain while kneeling and trying to surrender. As terrified men fled the building, they faced a gauntlet of armed white men led by police. Historians have totaled the dead at between forty and fifty, most of them Black men, with the total casualties easily reaching around 150.[6]

Incredibly, the president of the United States blamed Radical Republicans in Congress for the killings. During a speech in St. Louis in September 1866 he laid out a conspiracy theory that damned his opponents for planning a massacre. *They* had made inflammatory speeches that urged the Black population to arm themselves to shed white blood. The convention itself had been a sham; Johnson claimed it was illegal and intended to overturn the fundamental law of the state. These so-called victims had engaged in rebellion against a constitution recognized by the president. The Radicals caused this debacle, "and every drop of blood that was shed is upon their skirts and they are responsible for it."[7]

The two Republican members on the select committee investigating the massacre concluded otherwise. Their report stated that "rebels," "thugs," and disloyal men had elected the mayor, himself an unpardoned rebel. He had packed the police force with the same kind of unscrupulous men. They had instigated the violence. The president supported the wrong side. Nothing but military power could protect the safety, security, or peace of loyal men and women. This majority report of the select committee recommended that Congress intervene, passing legislation "to secure to the people of Louisiana a republican form of government."[8] This referred to the "guarantee clause" in the Constitution, as mentioned above, that empowered Congress to guarantee that representative governments functioned in the states. Moderates used the guarantee clause—as one historian recently observed— "as a way to justify the use of federal power to intervene in states of the former Confederacy."[9]

Republicans encountered continued evidence that, in addition to freedpeople, white Unionists and soldiers also suffered at the hands of former rebels. A select committee from the House had been charged by colleagues to visit South Carolina to gather the facts in the case of the murder of three Union soldiers. Although the incident had occurred in 1865, the final report came to Congress only in early 1867, in time to become part of the debate over military intervention. The victims had been guarding bales of cotton seized from a local planter. Close to midnight, six men had come upon the soldiers and ordered them to stand down so they could reclaim the cotton. The soldiers refused, so the assailants executed them. All three bodies tumbled into the dark waters of the Savannah River. One of the men had been alive when he fell; drowning finished him off. The attackers hurried from the scene, leaving the cotton undisturbed.[10]

What happened next was arguably more disconcerting. A military commission found four men guilty of the murders during a thirty-day hearing. They were sentenced to hang but eventually had sentences commuted to life imprisonment. Yet they went free in December 1866 because the Supreme Court—as part of a different case—had ruled that military trials could not occur in jurisdictions where civil courts functioned. The convicted men returned home, where civil authorities ignored the case and never initiated a prosecution. The inhabitants of the region greeted two of the accused with an ovation, with townsfolk staging what was described as a "general drunk." Northerners appalled by such behavior saw that lawlessness and disrespect for federal authority had become a cause for celebration.[11]

The congressional report contained the partisan squabbling over the true nature of violence in the South. First, the two Republican members of the committee strongly concluded that the military needed to intervene. They stated that for the punishment of a crime, "the courts cannot be relied upon where soldiers, Union men, or freedmen are concerned." Law enforcement was stacked against freedpeople. Neither magistrates nor jurors discharged their duties fairly. The representatives added that matters had not changed for the better since the close of the war "but rather for the worse." The material interests of the country as well as considerations of humanity demanded that the general government deploy its military forces.[12]

On the other side, Edmund Cooper, a Unionist representative from Tennessee, took issue with his colleagues, proclaiming military justice unnecessary and the violence unsubstantiated. In his minority statement in the report, he outlined what had become the standard procedure for denying murders and outrages by saying that no one furnished specifics. He noted that four generals had testified to the committee. "It is true that they mention, in general terms, that Union men, federal soldiers, and freedmen, were not safe in their departments," Cooper wrote, "but when asked to specify the number of cases, and the localities where they have occurred, and the names of the parties injured, within the last twelve months, they could only mention one case in the State of Tennessee, at Nashville; one in the State of Mississippi, at Granada; one in the State of Louisiana, on the road between Alexandria and Monroe; and not a single case in the State of Virginia, . . . and no case in North Carolina, Georgia, Florida, or Alabama." A few isolated cases occurring over long intervals in distant localities did not justify military rule, he concluded, especially since the war had ended and obedience to law prevailed.[13]

A Detroit newspaper saw it differently, showing that the supporters of military intervention had become increasingly aware of the kind of evidence needed to refute charges that Radicals manufactured accounts of violence. The writer applauded that the information in the report accurately detailed what had happened. This correspondent observed that the investigation into the murder of Union soldiers had revealed no new facts in the case, "but heretofore they have rested upon newspaper statements alone, and the Copperheads were at liberty to denounce them as false." What was different? "Now, we have a series of facts sworn to before the committee, and presented over the names of some of the best members of the House."[14]

The Military Reconstruction Act began its journey in the House in early January 1867, emerging as a bill with six sections that nullified state governments in the South, carved the region into five military districts, and forced voting upon the region without discrimination by color. It captured the mood of many Republicans by leading off in its first sentence that no adequate protection for life or property existed in ten Southern states. Most of the bill's narrative hammered that point home. Military officers were to stamp out disorder and violence, and they had the power to convene military commissions to fight criminal behavior. Congressman Thaddeus Stevens characterized the legislation as "intended simply as a police bill to protect loyal men from anarchy and murder."[15]

The Freedmen's Bureau data became part of the debate in the third week of February, after the bill had cleared the House. The information helped the Radical cause. It was at this time that Senator Henry Wilson stepped forward with his vest-pocket notebook, providing an extraordinary level of details on the murders and outrages that had been occurring in many parts of the South. The material offered advantages over prior lists of violence. It did not come from the partisan press, from anonymous observers, or from government reports framed by congressmen that, even if witnesses had been sworn to an oath, bore the taint of political bias. And it presented what Cooper had stated was missing in the testimony by the generals to his committee reporting on the murders of three soldiers in South Carolina: "the number of cases, and the localities where they have occurred, and the names of the parties injured."

Wilson's information spoke volumes about the lack of presidential initiative to enforce the Civil Rights Act. The senator said that since the law had passed in the spring of 1866, Southern whites had committed 375 murders and 556 outrages. Few if any were held accountable for this lawlessness. He listed totals of slayings and criminal activity in Georgia, Kentucky, North Carolina, South Carolina, Mississippi, and Virginia. He saved his most extensive reporting, however, for Texas. The senator confirmed that he had received the information from the Freedmen's Bureau. A couple of days earlier, Gen. Joseph B. Kiddoo, who was stepping down as assistant commissioner of Texas, had arrived to talk with Wilson, who then placed on record nine months' worth of murders and vicious assaults on freedpeople. Bureau officials in general had hurried to collect the information, and Kiddoo was among the first to get it into congressional hands. Not surprisingly, Texas held a prominent spot in Wilson's accounting of atrocities.[16]

The data from the Lone Star State appeared in the *Congressional Globe* under five columns: the month of the incident, the name/ description of victims (some could not be identified), the locality in which it occurred (generally the county), the nature of the outrage, and remarks that indicated whether any action had been taken by civil authorities (basically none). Wilson's list represented the most explicit accounting to date of atrocities, collected with the intention of public dissemination.[17]

The accounting startled a newspaper editor in Texas. The Freedmen's Bureau described incredibly brutal acts. One man was killed while herding sheep and then beheaded. Unknown "desperadoes" in Fannin County coldheartedly murdered three freedmen, declaring they simply "wanted to thin out" the African American population. Two other freedmen who had tried to take complaints to the Freedmen's Bureau agent were found dead. In Tarrant County, men dragged two women from a home, raped both, and murdered one of them. The editor recognized that such details "are the moving forces of Congressional action," which acknowledged the impact of the bureau's efforts. But the writer could not yet concede the accuracy of the reports. "Many of these cases have never been heard of by us," he said, adding, "We publish them, and ask that wherever there is any falsehood or misrepresentation that it shall be made known, and the State relieved of the odium of the charge." By enlisting his readers to deny the veracity of the reports, he had asked for the impossible.[18]

In revealing the findings, Senator Wilson underscored that the material documented only a fraction of the criminal activity, and newspapers made a point of explaining that the figures did not include the casualties from the massacres in Memphis and New Orleans.[19] A short deadline for gathering the data had not allowed for the fullest accounting. Yet another factor meant the atrocities were underreported: Southern whites intimidated the freedpeople against reporting violations. Wilson reproduced an account from Gen. J. W. Sprague, assistant commissioner for Arkansas, who noted that freedpeople received threats on their lives if they intended to detail wrongs to agents of the bureau, "and in many instances the persons making reports are missed and never heard of after. I believe the murders herein reported do not embrace one half the number that have been committed during the time mentioned."[20]

Within a few weeks, the government gained access to information on Louisiana that was equally damning. The communication from the Freedmen's Bureau personnel highlighted how early agents were in the process and how quickly they had tried to fulfill the orders of General Grant and Commissioner O. O. Howard to gather data, rushing it to friends in Congress. An officer on March 9 sent a tally of the murders and outrages committed in the state from the time officers had established themselves. The order triggering this report had come to him from Washington on January 24, or just days after Grant had asked Howard to furnish proof that Southern violence had escalated to the point of requiring martial law. It had arrived too late to be used by Wilson, but it underscored the need for urgent action. The Louisiana officer knew of at least 80 killed and another 210 shot at, whipped, stabbed, and beaten. All of the victims had been

Black. As for the number of African Americans who had murdered whites, there was only one. "In no instance in any of the foregoing cases," wrote the officer, "had a white man been punished for killing or ill-treating a freedman."[21]

This attention to detail in material gathered by military officers on the ground failed to persuade the opposition, who held partisan and racial biases. Black people faced an enormously difficult task in getting their voices heard about the injustice that they experienced, but an even greater task in having their stories accepted as true by the vast majority of white Americans.

A day after Wilson's data-filled report appeared, Senator James R. Doolittle of Wisconsin challenged its veracity. Although an antislavery man who had supported Lincoln, Doolittle had been a Democrat before adopting the Republican Party and was among the more conservative members on his side of aisle. That became obvious as he attacked the accounts of persecution of Union men and freedpeople as grossly exaggerated "and in very many instances absolutely, unqualifiedly, and wickedly false." Typical of the men who tried to discredit accounts of violence, he mustered his own examples from individuals he claimed were of unimpeachable character. He named them: a General Herron, who commanded the Department of New Orleans; a Colonel Mann, collector of the Port of New Orleans. He criticized Wilson indirectly by saying, "Mr. President, gentlemen say that they have reports from the agents of the Freedmen's Bureau, and reports from persons whose names they dare not read, and other authorities which they dare not mention. They talk of outrages by the hundred and by the thousand." This was, he claimed, a gross exaggeration. As for the soldiers who furnished the information, Doolittle dismissed them as men filled with ambition who provided outrageous claims to increase their own power over the South.[22]

Garrett Davis, a Democrat from Kentucky, joined the effort to discredit the information. He attacked both senators from Massachusetts, Wilson and Charles Sumner, for spreading false accounts. He blamed Sumner for reading letters reporting atrocities without naming the authors, hinting that the expressed desire to protect writers from retaliation hid the fact that they did not exist. Could the senator recount a case in which a person lost his life for writing such a letter? If not, then that proved freedom of speech existed. As for Wilson, Davis noted that the senator had provided a table of cases in which he said justice had not been administered. The number was very large, which Davis regarded as a fiction, too. He admitted that crime existed in the South, but such things occurred in all of the states. Cruelty was not exclusive to the former Confederacy.[23]

The main assault came from Senator Edgar Cowan of Pennsylvania, a conservative Republican who consistently fought his party's prescription for Reconstruction and had spoken out against the Civil Rights Act. He led his colleagues through an account of how Wilson's information had come to the Senate. It began with the inquiry to the president on January 8 to report on violations of the Civil Rights Act. He reminded his listeners that only the secretary of war had reported any, and those consisted of only a few cases. Yet Wilson "has a little book in which he has a catalogue of enormities that would have sunk Sodom and Gomorrah; he has them all ticketed down." He sarcastically said that the material provided "an exactitude to give you the most exact dimensions of crime in the Southern states, can tell you how high it soars, how deep it dives, its superficial measure, or its cubic quantity to a hair's breadth." The number of cases in Texas struck him as too incredible to believe. If this were the situation, then Black people would have fled the area, he said. That they stayed proved the accounts as false. He also considered it ridiculous that Wilson had information that the heads of the federal departments, save one, apparently did not. And as for the War Department, if it knew that many Black people had been murdered in Texas, why did it do nothing? Why, he asked, did no one try to save these people from being butchered? The answer to him, of course, was that the atrocities had not happened.[24]

It is worth stepping back to take stock of the parries and thrusts here. The information in Wilson's vest-pocket book had been shaped by the debate and also changed it. The information conveyed in a new way intelligence from the South to the public at large. Having concrete details departed from the anonymous letters of individuals often read by senators as evidence of Southern resistance. Wilson's approach caused opponents to adopt the same method—to quit using anonymous correspondence and to use names of sources to give their own pushback greater validity. Doolittle became adept at this, reading to the Senate testimony from a Northern legislator who left for Alabama, a Vermont man who did the same, a soldier who served in Texas, and a clergyman.[25] Detractors also attacked the motives of the other side, suggesting that soldiers who reported atrocities did so out of ambition to expand their power. Finally, they complained that the claims of outrages overlooked that violence was simply a part of American culture.

The sheer weight of evidence, however, supported the legislators who proclaimed the need for greater protection of loyalists in the South—partly because of its origins with military officers.[26] It was easy to ascribe dishonest motives when accusing soldiers as an abstract class, but when it came to individuals who were named, then reputations came into play. Congressman Timothy R. Howe, Republican of Wisconsin, put the matter into perspective succinctly. During the debate over Military Reconstruction, he brought up the New Orleans massacre, observing that "a government which murders does not afford adequate protection to life and property; and you must convict General Sheridan [in charge of Louisiana and Texas] of inaccuracy or falsehood or misapprehension, or you must agree that that government is guilty of murder."[27] Phil Sheridan was a controversial figure whose hard-nosed supervision of the region saw him removed from the post by Johnson, an action that helped lead to the impeachment of the president. But it was difficult to assault the general's commitment to his duty, his devotion to the Union, or his veracity.

On March 2, 1867, Congress amassed enough votes to override the veto of President Johnson to enact the Military Reconstruction Act. The legislation put the protection of loyalists in the South front and center.

Had Wilson's vest-pocket book made any difference? A few people had thought so at the time, but the bill likely would have passed anyway. Republicans dominated both houses, and they intended to seize the reins of Reconstruction from the president while addressing the persecution of loyalists in the South. But the reports of violence affected the course of Reconstruction by providing hard evidence of the need for martial law. The situation paralleled how fugitive slaves and formerly enslaved people shared their horror stories through the abolition movement, which helped bring on the Civil War. During Reconstruction, freedpeople in the South risked their lives to provide documented instances of injustice. Their testimony mattered. The details supplied through the Freedmen's Bureau boosted moderates' confidence that they acted in accordance with the Constitution. Various letters, memorials to Congress, and newspaper accounts had broadcast a sense of the precarious state of Black and white loyalists, but Wilson's intelligence came directly from military officers on the ground who vividly described the atrocities. The information, supplied at great personal cost by freedpeople, supported decision-making at a crucial moment.

As Congress wrapped up its business, Wilson decided to make what became a monthlong tour of the South. He wanted to clarify what legislators had accomplished with the Military Reconstruction Act and the steps that states needed to take for restoring relations with the government. He hoped to send the message that obedience to the law provided the swiftest course for reinstatement in the Union. The senator also entertained another goal—to ensure that the freedmen who were about to exercise the franchise voted Republican. Critics North and South tried to use the trip against him by claiming that his safe passage proved his own charges wrong and that even a contemptible Yankee could tour the region unscathed.[18]

Wilson served as the vanguard of Northern white and Black politicians and community leaders who traveled the South to encourage Black men to vote the Republican ticket. The campaign indicated how uncertain Northern politicians were about the political behavior of African Americans. Even sympathetic whites wondered if recently freed slaves could vote freely while former masters were committing murders and other outrages. To help rally African Americans to the party, congressional Republicans enlisted the aid of Black leaders such as Henry Highland Garnet and John Mercer Langston, the latter the president of the National Equal Rights League that had lobbied for the Fourteenth Amendment and Black suffrage. Southern critics defamed the speakers as a whole as "political pilgrims." They portrayed Wilson and the rest of the "vagabond fanatics" as worried that too much peace existed in the South and that Blacks and whites might vote together. Consequently, the interlopers needed to stir up trouble when calm supposedly prevailed.[29]

Before Congress adjourned, Wilson and his colleagues took an additional step to protect Black and white loyalists from intimidation. At the end of a military appropriations bill, Wilson added a section that disbanded the militias in the former Confederate states. These were not the paramilitary groups, sometimes called regulators, that operated ad hoc in the South but organized units sanctioned by state governments. As early as 1865, officers in Mississippi reported that the state militiamen went house to house to search Black people for arms, which they then confiscated. This was done ostensibly to recover weapons issued by the U.S. and Confederate governments during the war, but the militia carried out a far more extensive campaign of seizure by taking revolvers, shotguns, and other hunting weapons, designed to curtail African Americans' ability to secure subsistence and to defend themselves. The assistant commissioner of the Freedmen's Bureau in charge of the Southern District of Mississippi confronted the militia leaders, reporting, "We had quite a spirited discussion on the subject in which I claimed that a freedman has as much right to own a shotgun as any citizen of Mississippi; and that they violated the law if they deprived him of his property."[30]

The Freedmen's Bureau again supplied information to Congress, indicating that the practice continued—and in more states than Mississippi. Wilson had asked the bureau specifically for this evidence. Brev. Brig. Gen. James Thomas, an assistant to Commissioner Howard, provided extracts from reports of the assistant commissioners throughout the South about the organization of militias. The material led to the inescapable conclusion that they contained the potential to become pervasive.[31] Gen. Daniel Sickles in charge of South Carolina had prevented the organization of fifty regiments in his department. Wilson understood the danger of these groups, warning that the members "in nearly all cases are rebels." The men forming these units refused to carry the U.S. flag. "They are hostile organizations," Wilson said, "officered generally by men who have been in the rebellion."[32]

Wilson's effort stumbled briefly; phrasing in his first draft of the military appropriations bill called not only for disbanding the militia but also for disarming its members. This sparked criticism from a host of legislators, including sympathetic ones, who considered it an unconstitutional attack on the right to bear arms. To get his bill through, Wilson dropped the wording. The members of the militia had to disband, but the individuals retained their weapons. While eliminating a military organization hostile to freedpeople, the action left guns in the hands of people inclined to use them and irritated by the belief that federal power had wrongly forced them to stand down.[33]

Wilson traveled into the South in early April, confident that the Republican Congress had done its best to secure the safety of loyalists and that it had taken consequential steps toward supplying greater power to Black men for their own protection. He began with a speech at Petersburg, Virginia, on April 4. The receptions there and at Richmond encouraged him to make a more extensive journey, which he began mid-month. Lasting through early May, his itinerary carried him through Virginia, North Carolina, South Carolina, Georgia, Alabama, and Louisiana.[34] A majority of the crowds—sometimes estimated at around 5,000—consisted of African Americans. The white people who turned out tended to be Republicans, although some rebels attended and, at some point, even delivered speeches to try to counter the senator's message.[35]

Petersburg set the tone. Wilson delivered a speech that was surprisingly conciliatory, given that he self-identified as a Radical. But he was a forgiving man by nature. He stated that the war was caused by thirty years of conflict over human slavery. "On the one hand was a system of slavery, and on the other of freedom." For this, he said, the North shared the blame. Anticipating a stance that evolved over the next decades, he even commended Southerners for their bravery in battle. Both sides had met, Wilson said, on 625 battlefields, and Southern soldiers had fought with heroic valor. Strangely for a man who tried to convince his colleagues about the extent of atrocities in the South, he made no mention about the violence. His posture caused a Northern newspaper to tout this Radical as "the apostle of moderation" because he did not espouse vengeance.[36]

Wilson's travels backfired in one aspect, however, by giving detractors ammunition to deny the validity of the outrages he had articulated on the Senate floor. Democratic reporters noticed that even though Wilson delivered an inflammatory doctrine, his appearances provoked no violent reaction, which to them undercut his message about atrocities in the South. In other words, they saw the senator's safe passage as proof that anarchy did not grip the region. A Georgia newspaper wondered about the lack of attacks against him, asking whether he would "be good enough to inform the public how he reconciles the fact with his oft-repeated denunciation in the Senate that it was unsafe for a Northern man to go South, and to speak his sentiments would be to risk his life?" It added, "Let him go home or retract the slander." The *Richmond Whig* could not help but add, "His presence is a telling commentary on the atrocious slanders which have been uttered that a Union man's life was not safe in the South."[37]

Northern newspapers noticed the contradiction. The *Providence Evening Post* wrote that there was a time when a man of Wilson's political faith could not travel through "Dixie" safely without the benefit of luck—and even at that he could hardly have secured life insurance for the undertaking. But times had changed. The writer indicated that the war had cleared the political atmosphere, and from now on Northerners would enjoy the right of travel through the country.[38] A newspaper in Detroit reprinted an article from a conservative organ in New York that echoed Southern criticism that Republicans followed a questionable policy to travel through a region in "a fevered state of political transition." It would be strange, in this newspaper's opinion, if former rebels did not react violently to indiscreet speeches. The item blamed the political sojourners for instigating outrages.[39]

A strong rebuke of the political stumping came from a former member of Lincoln's cabinet, Montgomery Blair, who charged Radicals with subverting government in their "lust for power." During a political serenade in October 1867, the former postmaster general accused those of the opposition of fostering the mistaken notion that the rebellion still existed when it had long been suppressed. They did this to establish a military despotism to overthrow white government with Black rule. "To this end," he told the crowd, "they sent their emissaries to the South to create the riots which formed the pretexts for setting up the military governments now established there, and they are secretly organizing military forces all over the country, and will not long want pretexts to set up similar governments throughout the land." In other words, Radicals provoked unrest so they could employ military intervention to enhance their political base. They lied to fulfill their "unholy ambition."[40]

Blair's comments made for good political theater during a crucial election year in the North. During 1867, voters from twenty states cast ballots in elections in which Republicans lost ground. As the national Congress imposed Black suffrage on the former Confederacy, Northern states backed away. Attempts to extend the vote to Black men failed in Minnesota, Ohio, Michigan, Missouri, and New York. Connecticut Republicans lost the governorship and almost the legislature. Maine Republicans likewise fared poorly. Ohio and New Jersey saw former Republican houses turn Democratic; with the changes, Democrats regained the power to appoint the states' U.S. senators. It was not a total collapse; Republicans retained most major offices and majorities in most state legislatures, although the margin narrowed. But the elections blunted the Radical surge in Congress, effectively killing confiscation bills and delaying passage of the Fifteenth Amendment to ensure Black voting everywhere until after the presidential election.[41]

Democrats used the results to reinforce their claims that Radicals lied about atrocities in the South, twisting evidence of Southern conditions to attack support for Black suffrage. Any whiff of a decline in violence—such as with Wilson's Southern swing—heightened the

Democrats' claims. An Illinois newspaper curiously noted that after passage of the Military Reconstruction Act, little news came about persecution of Black people. It said that "we hear nothing about burning school houses, murdered freedmen, expelled unionists and the various catalogue of crimes that teemed in the radical press for months."[42] The *New York World* raised the specter of a race war fomented by Republicans—a common ploy by Democrats during elections. It claimed that "negro outrages" committed against white people terrorized the region, ironically calling for military action to suppress it. Much of the criticism was aimed at Northern political conditions, arguing that Democrats should reject extremism in their own backyard.[43]

Wilson's remarks to the Senate about atrocities in the South had struck a nerve. The reactions demonstrated how his statements, and those of his colleagues, had carried across the country and how the information from the Freedmen's Bureau made an impact beyond the Senate floor. His pronouncements, as well as those from other Radicals, angered the white press in the former Confederacy and informed arguments in Northern political campaigns. As for the lack of violence facing Wilson: it would have been foolhardy to attack one of the leading U.S. senators in the Radical camp, especially one who—although adhering to Black suffrage and limited disenfranchisement of former Confederates from voting and public office—promised to forgive former enemies and let them resume their political lives once the specific terms of the Reconstruction Act were met.

What happened if someone were less moderate in speech? That became clear with William D. "Pig-iron" Kelley. As he made his own tour of the South, the Radical congressman from Pennsylvania ran into trouble during his address in Mobile, Alabama. During debates on the military bill in February, after the Freedmen's Bureau information had come out, he made a point of listing outrages that had occurred in North Carolina. This gave the Southern white press an opportunity to argue that Kelley was inclined to tar Southern whites as violent before he came into their area to lobby for Black votes.[44]

Matters came to a head on May 14, when Kelley apparently heard someone during his speech cry out, "Put him down." It sounded like a death threat to the congressman. Unlike his colleague Wilson, Kelley did not mind confrontation. He declared that he had the Fifteenth Infantry at his back and, if that proved inadequate, the whole U.S. Army at his disposal to fend off assaults. As the speech progressed, some disturbance at the edge of the crowd prompted an arrest by police. An unknown person fired a first shot, and a broader volley broke out. At a certain point, members of the crowd turned their aim on the speakers' stand, causing Kelley to dive under a table for cover. The disturbance lasted for perhaps an hour, with the congressman ultimately escaping unharmed. Accounts varied about the number killed, but it seems to have been one white man and two Black men.[45]

As representatives of the Republican Party stumped across the South, military officers moved into the region to implement the Military Reconstruction Act. The law ordered the army to organize new governments that adopted Black manhood suffrage and ratified the Fourteenth Amendment. Voting became restricted according to loyalty, as registrars appointed by the military screened applicants based on which side they had supported in the war. Former Confederates howled about their disenfranchisement, saying it proved Radical intentions to subvert democracy. The more intrusive the government in eliminating white voting, the greater the case for the immorality of Republicans—if they had exaggerated the violence at the root of their policies. Consequently, Radicals downplayed the extent of disenfranchisement, while Democrats in the North and the South argued that it involved a widespread abrogation of rights.[46]

Voter registration became another form of information-tracking by the government—one that enlisted the aid of the Freedmen's Bureau officers stationed in Southern communities. The Military Reconstruction Act stipulated that the army establish boards of registrars to determine who could cast ballots. (This did not yet involve elections for political offices.) Voters would be deciding on two issues: whether to hold conventions to change the fundamental laws of states and, if yes, which delegates should accomplish the task. The stakes were high. A white-Black coalition formed in this manner would overturn the old power structure and leave many former Confederate leaders on the sidelines of dictating policy. A Second Reconstruction Act of March 23, 1867, aided that outcome by demanding that people take an "ironclad oath" of loyalty to the U.S. government, which demanded the applicant to swear he had not been a former public official who then held public office under the Confederacy, engaged in rebellion against the United States, or aided or abetted its enemies. Registrars had to take the same oath, which placed loyal men into these important positions for screening the electorate.[47]

Many Northerners would have resented the imposition of voter registration in general, much less the Southern version. It was still a fairly new procedure in American political culture. Massachusetts had instituted a registration system in 1800, and a few other states in New England followed suit, but it was not the norm. More typically, prospective voters showed up at polls with whatever documentation they had to demonstrate their residency, sometimes by proving they had paid taxes but more often by simply gaining a nod of recognition from one of the community leaders who hung around the precinct. The electorate viewed registration suspiciously, because it did not necessarily eliminate fraud but gave party managers greater control over who voted. Under registry systems, people often did not have to show up to have their names included on rosters; instead, precinct politicians generally handed in lists of voters they considered eligible.[48]

A system that raised suspicions of corruption under normal circumstances gained additional negative baggage for Southern Democrats because of the composition of the boards of registrars. The "ironclad oath" severely limited the pool of eligible people, leading officials to fill the three-person registry boards with discharged Union army personnel who lived in the South, Freedmen's Bureau officers, and Black men. Detested by rebels, the men on these boards enjoyed broad power to determine who voted. As Congress refined the system through a Third Reconstruction Act in July 1867, registrars could call witnesses and challenge a person's right to vote. The registrars could ignore an oath based on other testimony, rumors in the community, or their own intuition that a person had perjured himself about Confederate support. Some voters could be denied their ballot even as they stood at the precinct, ready to cast a ticket. No appeals could be made—none at least that might change the outcome in time.[49]

The military sought African Americans to serve on registration boards. In Virginia, Gen. John M. Schofield formed committees of three white and three Black men to qualify electors. In the Third Military District encompassing Georgia, Florida, and Alabama, Gen. John Pope used two white people and one African American. Gen. Edward O. C. Ord in Mississippi and Arkansas proposed using two former military officers, presumably veterans who had mustered out and lived in the area, and a loyal citizen—"when there is one." He doubted he could find enough white loyalists. General Sheridan, who oversaw the region's most violent areas of Texas and Louisiana, searched for two residents from each parish along with a tried-and-true ex-army officer living in the city. The racial composition was not specified, but a report from Maj. George A. Forsyth in New Orleans indicated that Black men were recruited and that they "should be selected from among the most intelligent and best [k]nown of their class."[50]

Truly, the bottom rail was on top. A now famous image in *Harper's Weekly* has captured the revolutionary transformation, with Black men placing ballots into a choice of two clear globes. But the image did not portray the extent of the upheaval, which likely included a Black man screening white men for participation in elections *before* they entered a polling place. This registration process accomplished the hard work of politics, enabling a greater number of loyal men of both races to determine how Reconstruction moved forward. As one Northern newspaper observed, "The work of registering is of greatest importance. It is the foundation on which is to rest the whole work of reconstruction." When Election Day came, the occasional Black man also could be found sitting behind the ballot bowl as one of the commissioners supervising the polling and potentially denying the right of a white man to vote.[51]

Being judged by a Black man who had once been enslaved may not have been one of the worst encounters for former Confederates. White Unionists were considered enemies, too. In Mississippi, an election inspector held in awe one of the registrars, a known Unionist during the war, for overcoming a disability inflicted by rivals. Brev. Maj. Thomas H. Norton reported that J. G. Owen served even though totally blind. Calling him a "most remarkable man," the major said the old man's eyes were put out by political enemies during the war as a punishment for his loyalty to the United States. Yet he apparently knew the possible voters in Forrest County and could recognize them by their voice or their footsteps. The major concluded that "there seems to be a sort of poetic justice in making him a judge of their qualifications now to exercise political rights under the government they attempted to destroy." Many of the white voters screened by Owen probably did not share the major's delight.[52]

Who was right about the impact of this screening, the Radicals who underemphasized it or the Democrats who saw it as more widespread? Trying to calculate the number of white men excluded from voting because of their Confederate past presents a challenge, complicated by uneven record keeping and the partisan designs to distort the outcome. Republicans wanted to avoid charges that they had "Africanized" the South, while Democrats did not mind boosting the figures higher to characterize Radical Reconstruction as an egregious overreach of powers by Congress employing undemocratic means to expand the Republican Party base. Recently, historians have downplayed the disenfranchisement of Confederates or, more often, paid it little attention at all. One study of voting in America dismissed the punitive measures as affecting perhaps only a few thousand white voters, with the restrictions temporary. In other words, they had little practical impact.[53]

The problem is that they did, but not necessarily in the obvious way and certainly not with the degree of callousness suggested by critics at the time.

The best guess at the numbers has come from William A. Russ Jr., a scholar who in the 1930s conducted the most thorough examination to date of the issue. He leaned heavily on material compiled by military officers published in the U.S. Serial Set, which contains House and Senate reports of investigations. In this case, Congress charged military officers to gather data on who voted and to make their best guess about the numbers disenfranchised by the Reconstruction Acts. Details came from both non-bureau military personnel and Freedmen's Bureau officers, putting the army in the position of serving as a fact-finding body for the legislative branch. The reports estimated that Virginia had disenfranchised 16,343 men; South Carolina, 8,244; North Carolina, 11,686; and Georgia, 10,500. These were the largest results; in contrast, Louisiana had only 2,169 white men prohibited from voting, and Florida a mere 350. Generals indicated that most of the figures represented strained estimates at best rather than hard numbers, given the deaths during the war and the difficulties in determining who stayed away from registering out of antipathy for the process. And five of the states supplied no information at all, further frustrating an attempt to assess the impact.[54]

The figures that exist suggest that registration, which could have allowed white enemies and former slaves to enact vengeance through arbitrary disqualifications of electors, instead proceeded with more due diligence than one might have expected. Despite flaws in the reporting—and the fact that five states did not share data— the number of disenfranchisements stated in the record came to roughly 50,000. We can bracket this figure with the upward estimate of 150,000 by historian James Ford Rhodes, which dealt with the men prevented from holding public office. As far as restrictions on white voting is concerned, the real number probably lies somewhere between 50,000 to 150,000, with estimates in newspapers at the time placing the figure at 75,000. In the 1860 election, more than 700,000 white men had cast votes in what became the Confederacy. The number of electors disqualified in 1867 does not seem like a figure that, by itself, overthrew the power structure of the South, although the process did target the rebel leadership and certainly was a factor.[55]

White disenfranchisement, however, must be considered in tandem with the enfranchisement of Black men as well as with voter turnout, for all made the difference in establishing Republican

TABLE 3.1. WHITE VOTING IN SELECTED STATES, 1867–1868

State	Registered	Failed to vote	Percentage
Alabama	61,295	37,159	61
Florida	11,914	10,491	88
Georgia	96,333	60,333	63
North Carolina	106,721	42,476	40
South Carolina	46,882	42,354	90
Texas	59,633	41,231	69
Virginia	120,101	44,017	37
TOTAL	502,879	278,061	55

Source: Senate Exec. Doc. No. 53, 40th Cong., 2nd sess. (1868).

governments. And here the white South contributed to its demise through a self-inflicted wound.

Because the Second Reconstruction Act of March 23 had stipulated that calling for conventions and ratifying state constitutions required a majority of the registered voters, the Southern Democratic strategy involved signing up voters but then boycotting the polls to disqualify the results. Overall, roughly 55 percent of whites who had registered turned out to vote, although this estimate can only be suggestive since it did not include all of the former Confederacy. The army furnished to the Senate completed information on voter turnout for only seven of ten states affected by the Reconstruction Acts. (Officers did provide white totals for registration but not for turnout for Louisiana and did not distinguish the racial composition of voters for Arkansas and Mississippi.) As table 3.1 indicates, in the areas identifying voting by race, the worst state was South Carolina, with 90 percent of white electors failing to vote. The best participation came in Virginia, with only 37 percent of registered white men staying away from the polls. Congress, however, realized the situation and ended this gambit by adopting a Fourth Reconstruction Act in March 1868. This changed the requirement for validating results to 50 percent of voters participating in elections, not 50 percent of who *could* vote.

The proof of the impact lay in the outcome. Registration that the Union army completed by November 1, 1867, resulted in barring enough antebellum political leaders from the conventions in which delegates rewrote constitutions for the South, and combined with boycotts by Southern whites, it enable the creation of progressive governments that conservatives hated. Northerners, Southern Republicans, and army veterans, along with African Americans, did the heavy lifting in forming the new governments. Black suffrage became ingrained in organic laws. The resulting constitutions carried out the Republican vision of free labor. They instituted public school systems and helped the poor with debt relief. They reformed voting procedures and encouraged business development. And they raised taxes to accomplish these things. The resulting legislatures also ratified the Fourteenth Amendment.[56]

Registration and disenfranchisement, though, left incredible resentment in former Confederates, whether they had been able to vote or not. Voting restrictions further deteriorated the reputation of the Freedmen's Bureau in the eyes of the white South because the military had staffed boards of registration and helped mobilize Black voters. The sting from a system that white Southerners castigated for overturning the racial hierarchy justified in their minds the increased use of terrorism against freedpeople. Those inclined to downplay the murders and outrages supplied by the Freedmen's Bureau excused lawlessness such as Klan activity as the expected by-product of misguided Radicals, who used "partisan excitement" and "exaggerated suspicions" to force unworthy Black people to govern over whites. According to one historian, "It made the white men among whom they must live their most bitter enemies."[57]

Critics at the time howled about how disenfranchisement allowed so-called ignorant Black men to vote when the "intelligent" leaders of the South could not. The *Charleston Courier* said the harsh federal measures that guaranteed Republican Party dominance proved that the real design "was neither Union or tranquility, but the perpetuation of party power." The Radicals, according to this item, wished to eradicate Southern institutions. The newspaper also excoriated the Republican missionaries who had come from outside, claiming them to be instruments of agitation, and criticized people like Wilson, Kelley, and a host of others who conservatives alleged created the violence in the South.[58] Racism shaped most assessments as white writers complained that the Reconstruction Acts had created a Black republic, "where the white man, if he can exist there at all, will have no rights which a negro is bound to respect."[59]

Northern Democrats eagerly embraced this interpretation, which became useful for political battles with Republicans in their own backyards. A Massachusetts journalist decried the imposition of military governments on the South, adding, "The result has been just what was predicted by Democratic orators and presses. The people were warned of the fraud that was being played upon them, but they would not listen." Concerning a Republican tract geared for the fall elections, the *New York Herald* alleged, "Under the specious cry of protection for the 'Unionists' of the South it justifies the disfranchisement of the white race and the elevation of the Southern negroes, who were rebels during the war, to political supremacy. In short, it is an unfortunate document for the party in whose interest it is written, and shows that it has no better weapons than violence and slang with which to fight its battle."[60] Items like this warned that the Republicans' egregious use of power—based on a lie—could happen in the North.

It did not take long for rebels in the South to use the imposition of martial law based on supposedly false information as one of the rationales for resisting the change in power. In Texas, it began during the summer of 1867, but by the spring of 1868 reports surfaced more uniformly from Freedmen's Bureau officers of assailants attacking men to affect politics. In Abbeville, South Carolina, four men broke into a home and destroyed Republican ballots that were to be distributed the next day.[61] A government report on the election in Arkansas during May 1868 noted that flying the U.S. flag on Election Day was met by a counter-flag soiled by feces and carrying an image of a Black person. Leaders in this same community of Jonesboro "are riding through this county exciting and assuring the weakminded that there will very soon be another war. They are also obtaining, so far as possible, the names of all persons for the ratification at the late election, asserting that their lives shall pay the forfeit."[62]

Boycotting elections, economic coercion, and other intimidation had failed to stop the momentum toward creating progressive governments in which African American men participated. A segment of the white South decided the time had come to increase the use of political terrorism, with the record of murders and outrages revealing the horrors that might otherwise have gone unreported in the countryside.

4

THE KILLING FIELDS OF 1868

As the Freedmen's Bureau continued to file accounts of murders and outrages in monthly reports, the military uncovered a horrible massacre of Black people in Louisiana. A bureau officer who had found an earlier description of deaths too incredible to believe stated more certainly that an estimated 100 freedpeople had been killed on September 30 and October 1, 1868. He went on grimly: "One instance mentioned where 9 freedmen were taken to [the] bank of Red River and told to swim for their lives, at which they plunged in and were shot as they rose to the surface. Another three freedmen making a coffin for one of their friends who was killed were brutally murdered." A different entry suggested that perhaps another 70 freedpeople had been killed at a different location in Bossier Parish. Other accounts placed the estimates of the dead much higher. At the time, no one could verify the exact details. When an officer attempted to inquire, assassins tried to kill him.[1] Well into November, the bodies of freedpeople from this and subsequent violent acts floated down the Red River as authorities tried to make sense of what had happened. State and congressional investigations followed.

What authorities learned through the testimony of surviving witnesses was terrible.[2] White people through the fall of 1868 had conducted mass executions of African Americans who had been tied, otherwise restrained, or lined up at gunpoint before being shot down. In Bossier Parish alone, the dead amounted to a state government–estimated 162, with the most recent scholarly assessment placing the murdered at 185 for both Bossier and Caddo Parishes. A list published by Congress in 1876 indicated that more than 200 Black people may have been slain during the spree of white violence in Bossier. We will never know the actual toll; even the best efforts of the Freedmen's Bureau could not identify all of the slain, and officers despaired of ever compiling a complete record. Undoubtedly more Black people were cut down than accounted for, making it possibly the worst case of atrocities in terms of body count committed during the Freedmen's Bureau's existence.[3]

Tensions over the 1868 presidential election had triggered the massacre. White people in this isolated area were not about to quietly accept the change in power wrought by Radical Reconstruction. And by no means had the massacre at Bossier and Caddo been the first or the last atrocity motivated by the era's conflict over Black political participation and the assertion of federal control in the region. Throughout the South, Black men had voted during 1867 and the spring of 1868, ushering in new constitutions that opened Black suffrage and public office to African Americans. Georgia and Louisiana voted Democrat for president when they had Republican majorities of registered voters, prompting the federal government to investigate why. They found that massacres of African Americans in the Red River region virtually eliminated Black voter turnout there. Murders and other intimidations limited Bossier and Caddo Parishes to one Republican vote each in precincts that had registered a total of 4,530 party members.[4] Along with other troubled parts of the South, the Red River region typified a decade-long arc of political violence throughout the former Confederacy that Southern white Democrats came to justify under the awful euphemism of "Redemption."[5]

The Freedmen's Bureau and military officers exposed the violence happening in rural areas that might otherwise not have surfaced and that laid bare the fallacy that it had nothing to do with political upheaval. It was a violence more deadly in body count than racial conflicts in cities such as Memphis and New Orleans. Black people here and elsewhere lived in agricultural zones that had been defined by slavery, where they might outnumber white residents. But these areas also were difficult for the overextended manpower of federal authorities to patrol because of their isolation and the complicity among white residents to condone the atrocities.[6]

Despite evidence of wrongdoing gathered by military personnel, the battle continued over the credibility of the information and the motivations of Republicans in reporting the details. Democrats launched a consistent stream of propaganda throughout the year intended either to dismiss the violence as a fiction concocted by Radicals or to blame the same people for leaving little choice for white Southerners than to defend themselves against threats to their liberties. Freedmen's Bureau agents serving as an investigatory arm of Congress identified a hazy new organization known as the Ku Klux Klan, which many Northerners denied existed despite the reporting. The efforts to track down and document murders and outrages filtered into local power struggles as Black politicians amassed whatever ammunition they could to convince the public and Congress that atrocities demanded greater military intervention, not less.

By 1868 the Ku Klux Klan had emerged as an increasingly visible element behind political terrorism. Historians locate the birthplace of the Klan in Tennessee, with outbreaks becoming more apparent in 1867. It entrenched itself in many parts of the former Confederate states, with the common goal to prevent Black people from voting. Democrats and other naysayers disputed the organization's very existence. Democrats skillfully played on racial notions to twist any unrest into the fault of Radicals trying to upset the established racial order.[7]

An apparent uptick in violence with a political purpose drew Congress's attention to Kentucky and Tennessee. These former slave states departed from the narrative of Reconstruction. Congress recognized Tennessee as rejoining the Union in July 1866; it thus escaped Congressional Reconstruction. Kentucky was a border state that remained loyal to the Union but, as many scholars have alleged, ostensibly turned wholesale Confederate after the Civil War. Its legislature failed to ratify the Thirteenth Amendment ending slavery.[8] Military intervention to protect loyalists was more difficult to justify ideologically and legally for these two states because the government recognized that civil authority functioned, including courts and the constabulary.

Uncertainty over the extent of violence in these states caused Congress to request information from Commissioner O. O. Howard in July 1868 on the atrocities that had been committed. As happened more frequently, the Freedmen's Bureau reported atrocities to the legislative branch, funneling intelligence gleaned by soldiers in communities. Documentation that named assailants and traced the individuals who had been slain found its way into the annual message of the president that November.[9]

Tennessee had been a troublesome state from the time it became "reconstructed." The rebels there vexed Maj. Gen. George Thomas, who supervised the region as part of his military department. Violence that intended to destabilize the Republican regime worried the governor as well as military officers. Thomas, a Union general who had been one of the top four officers under Grant by the end of the war, had seemed less concerned when he testified before the Joint Committee on Reconstruction in January and February 1866. Then, he had supported recognition of the state as having taken the necessary steps for reuniting with the Union. Congress agreed and restored the state by July 1866. Yet it did not take long for the general to change his mind. By 1868 he expressed fears that an insurgent, secret organization had formed to conduct terrorism against white and Black Republicans.

Freedmen's Bureau information supplied to Congress validated the concern. Samuel Mayes Arnell, a Republican from Tennessee, had requested the details. He asked specifically for the reports of Maj. Gen. W. P. Carlin, who supervised freedmen's affairs in Tennessee and Kentucky. Carlin reported that secret organizations operated in the Middle Tennessee counties of Giles, Marshall, and Maury. With its county seat of Pulaski, Giles has been credited by historians as the birthplace of the Klan. A letter from there in February 1868 portrayed the rebel element as bitter as ever: "If there is any change it is for the worse. Union whites and negroes are hated with a terrible hatred." Outrages occurred, with Black people dragged from homes at night and whipped to discourage their voting the Radical ticket. White Republicans also were targeted. Another Freedmen's Bureau report indicated that the groups caused great excitement and went under various names, such as Yellow Jackets and Red Caps. They traveled through the region seizing the weapons of African Americans and warning them to leave or be killed.[10]

Carlin, assistant commissioner for the bureau, detailed a Klan uprising that appeared in March in Murfreesboro, a little more than thirty miles south of Nashville. Most of the activity appeared to be threats rather than slayings—efforts to affect voting. Carlin bluntly stated that he believed "there is really a war of races constantly going on." He also arrived at a grim realization. Because the federal government acknowledged Tennessee as readmitted to the Union, he could not intervene because civil law held sway. The government did not send troops to handle disturbances unless requested by local officials—an unlikely scenario, he added, "as nearly all the county officers are ex-rebels."[11]

Carlin's fuller report in the annual message of the president in November 1868 explained why the incident reports of murders and outrages (detailed in chapter 2) had been so low for Tennessee when all knew that a far greater number had occurred. Officers essentially started their data collection from scratch in 1868, and the accounts assembled for Congress never made it into the record of the regular monthly reports of assistant commissioners. The Freedmen's Bureau, according to an army officer, "has never kept a complete record of the murders that have happened in the different sub-districts, and has had to gather the information from the courts." He added that those efforts had hardly gone smoothly. Local officials, many of them former rebels, rarely cooperated and more often than not had thrown obstacles in the way of gathering the information.[12]

These diligent efforts produced records of 162 people murdered in Tennessee from July 1, 1867, to July 1, 1868. Even with an accounting far from complete, this meant the state had the most homicides tracked by the bureau behind Texas and Louisiana and placed it in the neighborhood of Georgia. These were the crimes that could be teased from court records despite the foot-dragging of local officials. West Tennessee contained the worst violence, with ninety-eight slayings. This area included strife-torn Memphis. Next was Middle Tennessee, the region that gave rise to the Klan, with fifty-one killings. East Tennessee, an area with far fewer Black people and known as a Unionist stronghold throughout the Civil War, logged thirteen deaths.[13]

It was astounding how many of the perpetrators authorities identified. Only ten of the assailants were listed as "Unknown men in disguise," presumably the work of the Klan. Fully 80 percent, or 130, of the crimes were committed by people whose names were known and recorded by law enforcement. Some of the assailants had been arrested, but the vast majority went unprosecuted. Perhaps as noteworthy was that a majority of the dead, ninety-seven to sixty, were white, although the race of a handful had not been determined. Assuming all of them to have been Black still left a white majority.[14]

Kentucky in the same time period, from July 1867 to July 1868, had not generated quite the number of outrages. The Freedmen's Bureau there accounted for the murders of twenty African Americans and twenty-eight white people, or forty-eight total. In their compilation, the officers listed only nine of the attackers as unknown, with none of them mentioned as in disguise.[15] But the state also featured gruesome, targeted slaughter designed to send a message. In one case, assailants fell upon a white commissioner of registration while he worked in his field, tied his hands, and took him more than a mile away before riddling his body with fifteen bullets. The citizen who reported this to General Thomas said Union men were likely to be killed at any time.[16]

The collusion of law enforcement and the racial mix of victims underscored that political terrorism lay at the root of the outrages. In both Kentucky and Tennessee—at least according to the limited data scraped together by the bureau at the time—the murders of white people outpaced those of African Americans. This does not mean that no racial component lay behind the violence. Black people remained the principal focus for outrages, and there may have been a greater tendency among civil authorities for cases that made it into court records to note the murders of white people rather than the deaths of African Americans. Whatever the circumstances, white victims were in many cases Republicans (referred to as Union men) who supported the political participation of African Americans. They had to be dealt with. Terrorism fell upon anyone who threatened to upset racial, political, and economic hierarchies. Frightening, too, was how law enforcement in Tennessee looked the other way. Authorities had the names for most of the assailants, yet few faced legal penalties. Terrorists committed lawless acts without fear of punishment, despite officials knowing their identities. The majority of white people in those neighborhoods either felt helpless to battle the assailants or signaled their tacit approval.

As far as other regions of violence, Commissioner Howard in his annual account noted the usual hot spots of Texas and Louisiana. Fairly quiet were Alabama and South Carolina. Labor unrest percolated in North Carolina, where planters fired Black workers who engaged in politics, but little Klan activity happened there yet. Howard did describe outrages and personal abuse resulting from elections in Mississippi, but he considered the courts as functioning fairly reasonably. They could handle it. Arkansas concerned him, however. The administration of justice there had been far from effective. Arsonists torched three African American churches in Ouachita County in April, and the KKK had become active in various parts of the state, causing troops to be stationed at twenty-four different points. But because civil authority had been reestablished in Arkansas in late July, there was little the Freedmen's Bureau could do to help African Americans there.[17]

Howard also noted that in Virginia the sentiments of white people left "much to be desired with respect to a cheerful recognition of the rights of the freedmen as citizens." Although a minimal presence as yet, the Klan had appeared in reports from time to time as early as April 1868. The terrorists visited houses of Black men at night; in some cases they placed ropes around the victims' necks and threatened to hang them "on account of their political opinions." Howard added, "The object of these midnight demonstrations, which have been very rare in this State, appears to be to intimidate and control the freedmen in the exercise of their right of suffrage." Appearing in the reports of the Freedmen's Bureau was the backlash of Southern whites against the gains Black people had made during the early stage of Military Reconstruction. The bureau served as an important resource for exposing this ugliness.[18]

Conservatives, however, rejected the conclusion that white men declined to allow democratic rituals to function fairly. They refused to concede outrages as political in intent versus cultural in nature and just as often denied that they happened at all. In fact, Northern and Southern Democrats did their best to turn Radicals into the scapegoats for whatever unrest happened in the former Confederacy and to condemn their political opponents as the originators of a race war in which Black people allegedly committed outrages against whites.

Thomas A. Hendricks, a senator from Indiana and future vice president of the United States, advanced this interpretation in February as he criticized Military Reconstruction in a way that underscored that conspiracy theories have often played a role in American politics. Detractors like him condemned the Freedmen's Bureau for organizing Black people politically through Union Leagues or Loyal Leagues—Republican clubs that African Americans formed for political education, and sometimes self-defense, even before gaining the franchise. To Hendricks, the bureau had become a partisan operation and the leagues secret societies that operated like shadow governments conducting punitive courts against Black people who stepped out of line. He claimed that these secret organizations encouraged Black men to prevent a sheriff in Alabama from making arrests. He also quoted from an unidentified newspaper that a gang of "negro desperadoes" infested eastern North Carolina "committing nightly murders and outrages to such an extent that the people were completely terror stricken."[19]

This slant on racial violence thrived among Democrats in the North. Hendricks had plenty of company in espousing that Black people belonged to secret societies such as Union Leagues that outside agitators were using to incite a race war. In this view, Radical politicians were the chief conspirators, with the Freedmen's Bureau officers as their agents. The *New York Herald* accepted the notion that in ten "military provinces" of the South "a war of races is being fast fomented, leading to continual outrages at present." The columnist made the unsubstantiated claim that more Black people committed outrages on whites than the reverse. It declared that Black "supremacy" would never be accepted. Similarly, the *Daily Albany Argus* in New York alleged that Radicals used the Freedmen's Bureau to report one-sided accounts of white violence upon Blacks. It favored the reporting in the "established press of the South"—meaning white newspapers—that contradicted these stories with outrages by Black people. Further, the *Daily Albany Argus* foreshadowed a tactic used to prop up white supremacy through lynching later in the century: the newspaper cited attempted rapes by Black men upon white women in Kentucky as one of the defensible excuses for white violence.[20]

The selective use of government documents bolstered these theories. A newspaper in Maine, under the subheading "Pretended Outrage upon Negroes," alleged that frequent references had been made about supposed violence against Union men in Southern states. To disprove this, the writer dredged up the minority report from 1867 of Representative Edmund Cooper, who had dissented in the investigation into the three murdered Union soldiers in South Carolina. It repeated the congressman's dismissal of violence because the four generals who testified could not specify the number of cases, the localities of the incidents, or the names of the parties. Meanwhile, the criticism ignored the material subsequently supplied by the Freedmen's Bureau that had overcome these deficiencies.[21]

The *New York Herald* pulled out a bigger gun. With General Grant in the midst of a presidential campaign, the newspaper revived the general's letter from his hasty tour of the South in November 1865. The item mimicked a jury trial, pretending to call the general to the witness stand to report on the condition of the Southern states. Grant in his letter had stated that peace existed and that former Confederates stood ready to do everything required by the government. He had changed his mind since then, but that did not matter to this writer. "Either General Grant was grossly deceived," the item stated, "or else that is true. And if it is true he ought not to be President."[22]

Finally, scholarship has shown that public discourse between 1868 and 1873 never resolved the doubts Democrats expressed about the existence of the Ku Klux Klan. These reservations thrived despite government hearings conducted in the early 1870s that gathered a host of testimony detailing the repulsive acts committed by this secret society. Yet the idea persisted that the Klan represented the product of overheated imaginations. Southern newspapers denounced the "Ku Klux Klan Humbug," citing it as a youthful prank or denying that it functioned at all. Northern newspapers like the New York World supported such a position, as did Democrat politicians. One historian has marveled at how, despite a raft of information and hard evidence to the contrary, the national culture embraced the skepticism, with even Republican newspapers like the New York Times from time to time contributing to the notion of the Klan as a fake organization.[23]

The terrorism, however, was very real. Yet conservatives attempted to change the narrative of the cause of unrest from one of white terrorism supported by Democrats to lawlessness employed by Radicals and Black people.

The efforts at political terrorism achieved their goal only sporadically. Even Klan-infested Tennessee had not gone Democrat during the balloting for president in 1868. That honor among the former Confederate states belonged to Georgia and Louisiana, which demonstrated to conservative whites the rewards that political violence contained—and which the Freedmen's Bureau helped to expose.

White Georgia's blatant assault on Republican dominance began in the spring of 1868 as a group of men numbered at between twenty and thirty forced their way into a boardinghouse in Columbus. They had come for George W. Ashburn, a white organizer of the Republican Party, delegate to the constitutional convention, and champion of African American interests. He had rented a room from a Black woman. Arriving shortly after midnight at the end of March, the assailants wore masks, some of them blackened. Ashburn had a pistol, but the intruders killed him with a volley of ten to fifteen shots as he stood in the bedroom. One man knelt to fire a final charge into the body. A woman who lived in the home recognized a man whose disguise had fallen off as a "respectable and orderly young gentlemen." But because of death threats, the woman recanted her testimony at the coroner's inquest. The verdict, consequently, came down as death caused by parties unknown.[24]

Recognized as one of the first murders by the Klan in Georgia—although there had been lynching of Black people that had not attracted this level of interest—the slaying prompted an immediate reaction by the federal government. General Grant pushed for an energetic investigation by the army and the use of a military commission to try the case. Without political relations restored with the United States, Georgia remained under the control of Maj. Gen. George G. Meade, the hero of Gettysburg. The army settled on nine men to accuse for the murder, including a physician, a commission merchant, two policemen, a deputy marshal, and active members of the Democratic Party. Meade told Grant that he saw a connection between the disorder in his district of Alabama and Georgia and the secret organizations operating in Tennessee, meaning the Klan. He begged for more troops, which were sent.[25]

The controversy commanded public interest. It involved not only leading men of the community as the accused but also high-profile lawyers, including the former vice president of the Confederacy, Alexander H. Stephens. A U.S. soldier served as a witness, confessing his own involvement as one of the killers. He had been recruited by locals to join the Democratic Party. Despite his and other testimony consistently showing the perpetrators guilty of cold-blooded murder, the trial did not end well. It lasted from June 29 to July 24, when Meade ordered the proceedings closed after elections installed a Republican governor and the legislature ratified the Fourteenth Amendment. This supposedly met the qualifications for rejoining the Union and ended military rule. The accused were turned over to civil authorities to continue the prosecution, which of course did not happen. The freed men returned to Columbus as heroes. In the end, no one paid for Ashburn's murder.[26] A member of the constitutional convention had died mysteriously from pistol balls that no one seems to have fired.

The usual mixed reactions appeared in Northern newspapers. The contrarians diminished the guilt of the assailants, blaming the trial on the federal government's intention to force Radical measures on the state and coloring the testimony as being harshly wrung from prisoners tortured in sweatboxes—an allegation that Meade vehemently denied.[27]

Although the state ostensibly had followed the steps for recognition, matters deteriorated considerably, with information from the Freedmen's Bureau helping Congress overturn Georgia's restoration of political relations, pushing it back until 1870 in part because of the unrest that continued. Bureau officers revealed counties that earned particular notoriety. The murders and outrages record grouped incident reports by counties, showing the areas of conflicts. Most of the worst were located in the southwest toward Alabama or the Florida Panhandle, which featured heavy cotton cultivation and larger farms, as well as significant Black populations.[28] The counties topping the list of incident reports were Clarke (with twenty-six) and Thomas (eighteen). Others leading the lists of frequency of reports included Baker (sixteen), Greene (fourteen), Schley (thirteen), and Dougherty (twelve). With the exception of Greene County, these last were in the southwestern part of the state.[29]

Not all of this violence was election oriented, but some was, such as the September 26 attack in which three white men in Baker County dragged a preacher who was the president of a Republican club from his home at night, beat him, and shot him in the thigh. But a good deal of the tensions reported in other counties suggested struggles over labor and race relations typical of Reconstruction.[30] Even so, these conflicts contained political consequences. Planters needed a predictable labor force, and they resorted to coercion partly because of the success of Black people in establishing themselves on their own plots of land. The labor drain had been dramatic, with Dougherty County losing 16 percent of its agricultural hands, mostly

Black; Warren, 24 percent; and Greene, 16 percent. Economic independence not only provided autonomy to Black people but also closed off a potential avenue of voter intimidation.[31]

Little ambiguity existed about politics being the trigger for violence in one of the more well-known conflicts during Reconstruction in Georgia, the Camilla massacre.[32] The Freedmen's Bureau had been heavily involved in reporting the incident, with the army investigating and putting together an account under Meade's leadership. Data collected by the bureau also became important after the event as Black politicians used information on outrages to try to prove the discrimination against them in their bid to secure more federal help.

Understanding the origins of the dispute requires background into the eviction of Black legislators in September. When the new Georgia legislature formed in the summer of 1868, it contained thirty-two Black officials, twenty-nine of them members of the lower chamber. Conservatives tried to push through a resolution banning the Black members but failed, for the moment. When they raised the issue again, Republicans had split into factions out of antipathy with the governor. Those in favor of expelling the Black legislators claimed that the state's new constitution did not specifically authorize African Americans to hold public office. That much was true, but only because the wording simply left the matter unaddressed. The document implied that Black people enjoyed full political participation.[33]

Their expulsion prompted a continuing effort on the part of the Black legislators to fight for reinstatement. Under the leadership of Henry M. Turner—one of the ousted legislators, a former chaplain in the Union army, and a former Freedmen's Bureau agent—they immediately formed the Civil and Political Rights Organization and scheduled a convention of delegates for early October to unify their protest.[34] As the election season heated up, so did the strains between the competing forces.

On the morning of the collision, September 19, 1868, freedmen—estimated variously from 100 to 300—followed Philip Joiner, one of the Black members expelled from the Georgia General Assembly. The crowd intended to conduct a political rally for a congressional candidate and an elector who accompanied them. Some in the crowd carried arms, shotguns with one or two rounds. As the crowd neared the courthouse in Camilla, a white man came into the picture. "Jimmy" Johns, a dangerous man frequently in trouble and just as often drunk, waved his double-barreled shotgun at musicians in a wagon, ordering them to stop. They did so temporarily, but when they resumed, Johns became agitated and fired.[35] Black men fired back, often disarming themselves by discharging their load of buckshot. It may have been a trap: they were no match for the white people stationed around the square with a cache of loaded weapons handed out of buildings so men could continue firing. The procession scattered, with some heading for a swamp and others for woods as white men gave chase. The Freedmen's Bureau immediately reported twelve dead, and perhaps double that amount wounded.[36]

The massacre increased the incentive for Black legislators to fight for reinstatement, using information from the Freedmen's Bureau to help their case. From October 6 to October 8, they held a convention at Macon that drew perhaps 180 delegates from across 100 counties. The convention followed the lead of the bureau by creating its own committee to gather information on murders and outrages. Congress also wanted to learn more about what had occurred in Camilla, and the Joint Committee on Reconstruction called, among others, Henry Turner to testify in December. Did he know of atrocities that had been committed in Georgia? Yes, he replied, adding that if he had known he would be asked to make a statement about the condition of Black people, he would have brought the synopsis about violence prepared from letters and reports. "I could have laid before you an immense mass of documents on that subject."[37]

One petition in the congressional investigation highlighted the importance of the Freedmen's Bureau in amassing information. In early December, Philip Joiner and Robert Crumley sent a memorial to Congress asking for greater protection from the government. Joiner was the expelled member of the state legislature who had escaped injury during the confrontation at Camilla. Crumley was a Black pastor of the African American Methodist Church. Both men were from the Second Congressional District, where Black people faced worsening conditions. Once military supervision had been replaced by civil authority in July, outrages had escalated.[38]

The men knew of forty-six murders or attempted murders from January to March 1868 in which none of the assailants were punished. Joiner and Crumley had harvested this information from the Freedmen's Bureau. They added, "We have been denied access to the reports of the bureau agents covering the period from which to quote in substantiation of the above; but they are on file either in the sub-assistant or assistant commissioner's office, and doubtless will more than prove what we say." In other words, they had the bare-bones statistics but not the underlying descriptive material. That they made a point of identifying the source of this information in their petition demonstrated how important the bureau had become for substantiating cases of atrocities.

Even without supporting narrative, the numbers demonstrated the consequences of easing military oversight of civil affairs. The sub-assistant commissioner had recorded seventy-two cases of outrages occurring in August, the month after the initial readmission of Georgia to the Union. By the fall, Black people faced murder by the Klan for voting their consciences. Violence had been effective. During the presidential election, the Second District tallied a 7,000-vote Democratic majority when there should have been a Black majority of 8,000. For the entire state, the bureau reported 336 incidents of murders and outrages between January 1 and November 15, 1868—a mixture of murders, attempted murders, beatings, stabbings, and whippings. The details of perpetrators and victims mentioned by Joiner and Crumley made it into the congressional report.[39]

As happened throughout Reconstruction and beyond, conservatives mounted a vigorous campaign to discredit atrocities as exaggerated for political purposes. In this case, newly elected congressman Nelson Tift tried to convince the Reconstruction committee in the U.S. House that citizens in the state, whether white or Black, received equal treatment before the law. Northern-born Tift had spent much of his life in the South, settling in southwest Georgia, a region of intense racial conflict. He embraced the ethos of a slave society and served terms in the state legislature. The House Committee on

Reconstruction met in January 1869 to begin considering, among other things, whether to seat newly elected representatives from the state or to deny them recognition, with Congress also potentially reinstituting martial law. To influence a favorable decision for Georgia, Tift tried to prove that the legal system there functioned fairly for all residents.[40]

Tift created a survey that he sent to judges of the supreme, superior, and ordinary courts, as well as mayors of cities: a series of eight questions that dealt with whether laws were impartially administered, whether there had been organized resistance to Reconstruction, and whether officers of the law fulfilled their duties. He asked about the treatment of white people toward Black people, toward white Republicans, and toward Northern men who settled in the South. Did his respondents see any reason for the proposed renunciation of the present government and the reestablishment of military oversight?

Not surprisingly, the responses came back with a resounding "no." Tift collected and sent to the committee on Reconstruction in the House nearly 100 letters from jurists and legal officials from throughout the state. To a person, they declared that they upheld the law and administered justice fairly. A judge on the superior court from Atlanta gave the rare honest statement that the feeling toward white Republicans was "very bitter and very unkind." He added, "A systematic effort has been made to mortify, to slander, to disgrace, and to drive from society and from business, all white men who were open and avowed in their support of republican principles." Nonetheless, he blithely maintained that no Democrats had committed violence on white Republicans when it had, in fact, happened—if not in his jurisdiction, then elsewhere. Independent of politics, he believed that sentiments toward Northern men settling in Georgia were "perfectly kind." Like the rest of his colleagues, this judge erroneously portrayed Black people as committing more outrages against white people.[41] Tift's survey was akin to asking thieves if they owned the property they were suspected of stealing, then taking their uncorroborated word as the truth.

In such reactions, placed on record in congressional documents, can be found part of the evidence that eventually appeared in negative histories of Radical Reconstruction by academic historians from the late nineteenth century to the middle of the twentieth. The pushback organized by Tift provided fodder for the denial among scholars before the 1960s about the atrocities of the period—a denial that could be based on "evidence," or the unqualified use of direct testimony of a wide range of supposedly upstanding members of the judicial system. These were white men of note. Their word mattered to most white people more than the testimony of African Americans.[42]

Republicans, however, overlooked the attempt at misinformation from white conservatives. They were helped by a ruling of the supreme court of Georgia in favor of the Black legislators' right to hold public office. In March 1869, the U.S. Congress refused to recognize the new congressional representatives from Georgia, and then reinstituted military rule in December. Gen. Alfred Terry launched in January 1870 a purge of former Confederates from the legislature, replacing them with Republicans who had come in second place during the prior election. Restoration to the Union waited until July 1870. Violence documented by the Freedmen's Bureau, and the military in general, had reinforced the rationale for maintaining the heavy federal hand.

A massacre of Black people in Bossier Parish, Louisiana, started at the end of September as a white man from Arkansas named Gibson passed through on his way home from trading in Shreveport. He stopped at Shady Grove plantation, ostensibly to buy corn. When he saw a Black man nearby, he yelled, "You was all damned radicals." Other versions had the intruder asking the man if he was a Radical, but all accounts agreed that the Black man made it known he was a Republican. Once discerning that the Black man would vote Republican, Gibson leveled his weapon and opened fire. So began one of the larger outbreaks of atrocities anywhere against Black people during Reconstruction.

Matters escalated quickly. Gibson missed his mark. Black men rallied, captured the white man, and bound him—one account says in chains. They sat him under a tree, where he told them that he had intended to start trouble when coming to the place. News spread. White people came to free Gibson, which they accomplished. Somewhere along the way, two white men were killed, presumably by African Americans, although the record is not clear. By the next morning, it became open season for killing Black people—what even the Freedmen's Bureau record bluntly referred to as "the negro hunt."[43]

A number of the white vigilantes went back to Shady Grove to fire indiscriminately on freedpeople. They immediately shot down eight men and two women. A survivor added, "The women were killed for pleading for their husbands." The raiders, who included leading planters, then took seven men to a neighboring place at Gum Springs. There they killed six. One who was shot survived, but when the attackers heard this, they went back to the plantation and gunned the man down. They killed his wife, too.

The slightest gesture or accidental encounters proved fatal for Black people. At Gum Springs, white men came upon a Black man who refused to doff his hat; they put a chain around his neck, cut his throat, and hanged him on a tree, where he was left for three days. People feared to cut him down before then. In another chance encounter, as noted in this chapter's opening, Black carpenters who crafted a coffin for a slain acquaintance were murdered by white men who happened upon them.[44]

Although the Freedmen's Bureau report suggested most of the killings took place over two days, other testimony indicated it lasted for weeks. The record is unclear on this point, but the longer time frame is more likely correct. Refugees gave fearful accounts of wholesale murders where workers on plantations gathered in a row to hear their names called for the "death list." They were marched to Gum Springs and executed. One man on the plantation put it succinctly, "They thinned us out thin." Henry Ellison saw two Black men bury the remains of a man, woman, and their four children—bodies that had floated down the Red River in a bagging sack. They were neither the first nor the last bodies to make that journey. Henry Johnson, who sustained a wound to the head but escaped, said, "My old father, Robert Johnson, sixty years of age, was half hung because he voted the radical ticket. They said he was too old to kill, but they would just hang him a little anyhow to make him know better by the next election." His father never fully recovered from the injuries. After the massacre, whites apparently kept a "dead list" of those who escaped. They employed a sheriff to track them down and kill whoever he found. He succeeded at least once, shooting a man in cold blood and proving again that local justice was not on the side of African Americans.[45]

Other survivors related similarly terrifying experiences. The Freedmen's Bureau report contained the brief story of Henry Jones, who, during the Bossier violence, had been shot in the shoulder and feigned death to fool his attackers. The assailants then threw him between two logs, piled rotten wood on top, set it on fire, and left. He suffered severe burns but lived as he managed to crawl out from under the conflagration. Meanwhile, two Black men fearful for their lives dodged violence by occupying holes that they had dug four feet into the ground. They covered the holes with boards, topping them with earth and leaves for camouflage. They used this makeshift refuge for three weeks before they felt safe to emerge.[46]

The violence in Bossier was part of increasing intimidation in various portions of the state, but no region was deadlier than the Red River region, where the homicide rate quadrupled that of the nearest competitor.[47]

Spurred by reports of atrocities, the Republican-led general assembly for the state of Louisiana completed two joint committee investigations into the murders and outrages in the state, released within four months of each other. The first one had wrapped up in September before the outrages in Bossier and Caddo were committed. Legislators reopened the inquiry and in January 1869 released a supplemental report compiled through further examination of witnesses.

The second document in particular, which included the Bossier massacre, showed the heavy footprint of Maj. Gen. Edward Hatch, the assistant commissioner of the Freedmen's Bureau for Louisiana. The first tally by the legislature completed in September placed the murders in the state at 204. The second report, lifted primarily from the Freedmen's Bureau data released by Hatch, stated that in the months spanning September through November 1868, another 297 slayings had occurred. No one considered the information perfect because of intimidation of witnesses. "In some of the most violent parishes," the committee observed, "the terrorism has been so great that no testimony has been received from them at all." The committee believed that the number of murders in the state may have reached 1,000.[48] That estimate may have been too high, but it was hard to get a handle then, as it is now, on the number of the dead.

The slayings in Bossier Parish made up a majority of the cases, with Hatch's information placing the total dead at 162, or more than half of the atrocities committed from September to November. He also confirmed what historians have generally concluded by claiming Caddo Parish was the second most deadly parish, with forty-two murders. This is in the neighborhood of the numbers compiled by historian Gilles Vandal, who went through the effort of combing through numerous local newspapers to come up with his own total of 185 dead for both parishes.[49]

Vandal also noted that mass executions were common. In the scenario that opened this chapter, nine Black people were taken to the Red River on October 1 and told to swim for their lives but were killed as they came to the surface. Thirty Black people were taken from around Shreveport that same night, tied with ropes, and executed from behind. On October 12, seven Black people were chained in an abandoned building, which murderers burned down with the victims inside. Five Black men were taken from their work at a brickyard, marched to the Red River with hands tied, and then executed.[50]

Bossier and Caddo were not the only places where African Americans faced brutality. The Louisiana Joint Committee in its 1869 supplemental report focused on four areas of conflicts. In addition to the Red River region, political clashes occurred in New Orleans (September and October), St. Landry Parish (September 28), and Jefferson Parish (October 23).

In New Orleans, a procession by Republicans on September 22 prompted opponents to fire into the crowd. White people reportedly paraded in front of the residence of the commanding officer of U.S. troops bearing flags with the words "No Quarter." They tried to provoke a general killing on the pretense of Black people rioting. Fortunately, the violence ebbed quickly. Late in October, however, white people fired upon another procession, supporting the presidential campaigning of Grant and Schuyler Colfax, in which Black people lost their lives. African Americans went home, gathered weapons, and fired at their assailants. Unrest continued from Saturday night until Wednesday. Possibly seven white men died. The number of Black dead was at least thirteen and probably higher.[51]

St. Landry Parish featured an attack on freedom of the press. Also known as the Opelousas massacre, the killings originated with three men who on September 28 brutally beat a Republican newspaper editor named Emerson Bentley. Unhappy with what he published about a political meeting, the attackers came to the schoolhouse where Bentley taught Black children. One of them, a constable for Opelousas, stood guard with a pistol at the door while another beat Bentley with a cane. They then pulled out a document for the editor to sign, which professed to be a statement from Bentley that he had lied in his reporting. More blows caused him to comply, and the men left. Because Bentley taught Black schoolchildren, African Americans were angered by rumors that the editor had been killed. They put up resistance. White people fought back and took perhaps twenty-nine prisoners. The next night, all but two of the prisoners were taken out and shot dead. Remarkably, Bentley survived as he fled the area.[52]

One last outrage is worth mentioning because it resonated across the North. On October 17, men calling themselves the Seymour Knights, in reference to Grant's Democratic opponent in the presidential campaign, brutally murdered Sheriff Henry Pope and Judge Valentine Chase at Franklin in St. Mary Parish. The pair had been conferring outside one of their rooms on the second floor of what was described as a hotel or a tavern. The attackers ascended an outside stairway from the alleyway and opened fire. Pope died immediately. They hit Chase twice but not fatally. They shot him again as he fled the hotel, managing to run a little way before falling from loss of blood. The body of Pope, who had been a soldier in the Thirty-Third Illinois Volunteers, was taken back to Illinois for burial, where residents passed resolutions declaring the murder the work of the traitors who had tried to overthrow the republic by armed rebellion. No one faced justice for the killings.[53]

When the new governor of Louisiana tried to convince the federal government that he needed the military to remain in the state as a police force, the news caught public attention and elicited further controversy over the truth about atrocities. Republican Henry C. Warmoth wrote President Johnson in early August about the lack of protection in courts for many citizens. According to Governor Warmoth, "Men are shot down in roads, in their homes and elsewhere, without a question being asked or any steps taken to bring offenders to justice." A judge refused to hold court in the parish of Franklin without military protection, and a sheriff of the same parish, a Democrat, resigned because he had no ability to arrest or discharge the duties of office. "From the very best information, Mr. President, I have no doubt that 150 men have been murdered in Louisiana in the last month and a half," Warmoth wrote. Secret organizations that existed with the purpose of influencing the election outcome also had intended to assassinate the lieutenant governor and speaker of the state house—a plan thwarted by the presence of U.S. soldiers. Warmoth begged for more troops.[54]

Reactions in the press fell predictably along partisan lines. The *New York Tribune* and *Cincinnati Daily Gazette* took the report seriously, with the latter reprinting clippings that included Bentley's account of the violence at St. Landry and the murders of Pope and Chase. The *Gazette* also lifted material from the first report of the Louisiana legislature, which included a tabulation of 204 murders committed—all of this gathered before the Bossier-Caddo massacres became known.[55] But the *New York Herald* was having none of it. It printed an account from an unidentified correspondent who toured Louisiana in late August, proclaiming that the isolated nature of the geography lent itself to frontier justice, with bitter family feuds, "secesh animosities," and "unscrupulous rascality" on the part of Northern carpetbaggers. The writer concluded that Warmoth's 150 murders may have rested on a groundwork of truth but contained "a superstructure of very unnecessary exaggeration."[56]

The day before the presidential election, the *New York Tribune* ran a sampling of the violence in Louisiana, calling it "The New Rebellion." The report included a letter from an "independent Republican," who was not identified. The writer repeated information about the riot in New Orleans in late October and provided background on the slain Judge Chase. He also described a reign of terror in Louisiana in which Black people risked death if they went to the polls.[57] Anonymity of the letter writer made sense and probably was prudent for safety's sake, but it also was the kind of account that raised skepticism among Northerners about stories of violence. By not naming the accusers, the item opened itself to dismissal as a fiction created by Republicans.

Newspapers in the North continued to debate the reality of the outrages. One disgusted Republican editor in Connecticut printed the accusations of a rival editor that the reports represented a Radical campaign strategy. The Democrat asserted that Radical papers complained of outrages during the eight weeks prior to the election, adding, "But on the 3d of November they ceased, and we hear no more about them." This caused the editor of the *Connecticut Courant* to sputter, "Just see what stuff the man prints! He has readers who believe even that, but he ought to feel ashamed to send such fibs to intelligent men." He added that even Democratic accounts noted the massacres of people at Camilla and St. Landry's Parish. "Of course he knows all this," said the Republican editor about his rival, "but is he not editing a Democratic paper?"[58]

Conservatives typically characterized white violence as self-defense against Black people. This reflected the stance of the minority report in the second investigation the joint committee of the Louisiana legislature issued after the election violence of 1868. The lone objector admitted that outrages and fraud had taken place at the recent elections—this much was hard to dispute. Acknowledging that *some* bad episodes had occurred bolstered the credibility of those who decried the violence. Then the lawmaker claimed that in many instances Black people "committed brutal outrages, sparing neither age nor sex, having been taught to believe by their white leaders that they were better than the white people of the State, and entitled to more consideration by the Government." Republicans provoked the lawlessness by portraying whites as rebel traitors who deserved punishment. "The white people have had reasonable grounds for fear of an insurrection," he continued, "and they no doubt prepared themselves the best they could to protect themselves and innocents from violence and harm." According to this legislator, the solution for the problem was for "the white people of the State [to] be left alone to manage their own internal affairs."[59]

This attack on the validity of atrocities suffered from vagueness—in fact, the same lack of detail that Democrats often said was employed against them. Rarely did any of the rebuttals try to substantiate statements with dates, names, and incident reports similar to those amassed by the Freedmen's Bureau. If Democrats did use documents, it was to cite a minority report in a government record or to portray one episode that became extrapolated as a universal example. Unsubstantiated rumors of "negro riots" or potential armed action by Black people against white people provided convenient triggering mechanisms for white violence.

Democrats and white supremacists, though, rarely claimed that the names of victims and perpetrators collected by military officers were inaccurate. One has to search hard to find anyone contesting the details *within* the incident reports of the Freedmen's Bureau. Most of the time, opponents ignored the data that had been accumulated and instead attacked the motivations of the military officers who had collected it and of the public officials who used it as a basis for implementing policies.

The material on atrocities in Louisiana had a utility for Republicans in Congress even eight years later as the nation faced an electoral crisis. The reports from the Freedmen's Bureau—and testimony that appeared in the section of the Louisiana inquiry prepared by Republican lawmakers—had a second life in the wrangling over who won the 1876 presidential election. Republican Rutherford B. Hayes faced off against Democrat Samuel J. Tilden. The Democrat won the popular vote, but twenty electoral votes were contested from Florida, South Carolina, and Louisiana. For months, the nation did not know who would succeed Grant in the White House.

Controversy arose in Congress over the use of troops by President Grant—whether they had interfered in elections—and also over a board that had been established in Louisiana during Reconstruction to supervise elections. Democrats were suspicious that the federal government had allowed troops to meddle in elections and disputed the claims that election violence had a long history dating at least to the 1868 election.[60] In early December in the midst of this crisis, Fernando Wood—former mayor of New York City and by this time a Democratic congressman—introduced a resolution asking the president to transmit to the House copies of orders involving the use of the army in Virginia, South Carolina, Louisiana, and Florida. Virginia's senator suspected the army of meddling in his state's election. Meanwhile, the government investigated the other three states for election tampering.[61]

On January 24, 1877, the executive branch sent to the House a printed document of more than 500 pages that outlined atrocities that had occurred in the designated states since Reconstruction. Some of it dated back to the end of the war. Titled "Use of the Army in Certain of the Southern States," it contained military orders, tabulations of murders, and data on elections that showed the influences of the Freedmen's Bureau and other military records in tracking murders and outrages in the South. It also contained the testimony gathered by the joint committee of the Louisiana General Assembly in its investigation of atrocities during 1868. And it offered new information that postdated the disbanding of the Freedmen's Bureau, identifying leaders of the White League in Louisiana, among other details.[62]

Particularly useful to historians who study violence during the Reconstruction era are the tabulated columns of murdered and assaulted people toward the end of the document. The material appeared in the format pioneered by the Freedmen's Bureau, with columns containing names of victims, names of perpetrators, descriptions of outrages, and remarks. The bulk of it had, in fact, come into being through the bureau's efforts. For Bossier Parish, the columned material showed that 207 people had been killed. Unfortunately, there was no differentiation made for time of year (such as September through November), which made it impossible to attribute all of these deaths to political terrorism around Grant's election. But at least sixty-eight were identified as part of the Bossier massacre or proclaimed to be killings conducted on Shady Grove plantation, the epicenter for the slaughters. More scrupulous procedures in record keeping likely might have attributed more of the dead to that event.[63]

The best testimony for the credibility of the material came from the lack of interest by Democrats in the House in using the information. Numerous killings and intimidation of voters had occurred over the years—Louisiana likely had not had a fair election for quite some time. If anything, the document made an ironclad case for greater federal intervention during Reconstruction, not the reverse. After the "Use of the Army in Certain of the Southern States" went to Congress, Wood and his colleagues apparently ignored it. At least, they did not put it to use. The facts did not prove what they wanted to hear.

The hot spots of Georgia, Louisiana, and Tennessee all showed the impact of the bureau as it worked in tandem with military commanders sympathetic to curbing lawlessness. Texas, however, tells a different story of frustrations among state Republicans who turned to amassing information on atrocities in a public battle with a conservative general who refused to see the outrages occurring on his watch.

5

THE PROBLEM
OF TEXAS

When he arrived at Galveston in April 1866, Maj. Gen. Philip Sheridan had just completed a tour of a portion of his military district. The general presided over Texas and Louisiana, the two most murderous states in the South during Reconstruction. He was tired and dirty. He had no time to wash the sand from his face before people tried to engage him in conversation. One person in particular kept pressing the general for what he thought about the region. Sheridan did not disappoint. Blunt by nature, he was quoted as saying, "If I owned Texas and Hell, I would rent Texas and live at the other place." The person who asked the question turned out to be a reporter, and the news spread. Although Sheridan described the Lone Star State and the devil's home as if they were separate domains, to many white Unionists and freedpeople at the time, Texas and hell seemed like one and the same.[1]

Texas was in a class by itself in accounting for 57 percent of all the incident reports collected by the Freedmen's Bureau, but it also was unique in featuring a highly publicized clash between Radicals and a military officers over the reality of violence in the state. Unlike most army commanders who supervised Southern states during Reconstruction, Gen. Winfield Scott Hancock, a successor to Sheridan, refused to acknowledge the outrages occurring under his watch.

Unionists who came to power in 1868 adopted the reporting techniques of the Freedmen's Bureau to fight not only rivals but also Hancock. The Republican governor worked with a committee from the constitutional convention to circumvent the general to prove to Congress that the level of violence required continued martial law. The committee's report told a "frightful story of blood." It pushed back against those like Hancock who dismissed the statistics on crime, saying they represented "the facts, which cannot be suppressed by denials, or by denouncing them as fabricated for a political effect."[2]

Federal and state estimates had difficulty capturing the lawlessness with precision, partly because of the size of the state and the complicated nature of the violence, some of it unrelated to the upheaval from emancipation. Violence west of Austin, an area referred to as the "frontier," featured Anglos encountering Native Americans; along the northern border, outlaws galvanized clashes between white Unionists and former Confederates; and in the south, Anglos jostled with Mexicans. The settled regions by the time of the Civil War were larger than Mississippi and Arkansas combined. The state's scale outstripped the efficient reach of law enforcement or the U.S. military after the war. At best, the Freedmen's Bureau could document atrocities in roughly 60 out of 152 counties.[3] The horse stealing, saloon brawls, outlawry, blood feuds, and Indian conflict offered conservatives a plausible counternarrative to the claims of outrages as politically motivated and gave them enough leverage at one point to affect the distribution of soldiers. Although historians have come to accept the validity of Freedmen's Bureau reporting, even they have wrestled with whether a monocausal explanation adequately captures the causes of racial violence.[4]

The statistics from the Freedmen's Bureau, however, strongly support that political struggles underlay a bulk of the atrocities.[5] The data also show that political terrorism flourished in the settled regions containing the greatest concentration of wealth, as well as in a place of governmental power. Travis County, which contained the state capital of Austin, had the largest number of incident reports at 124. In its tracking through 1868, the bureau also cataloged racial violence in the eastern portion of the state, or the area most enmeshed in cotton production. East Texas was also the site of a transplanted slave society along the Brazos and Colorado River basins. Anglo masters during the 1830s had imported chattel illegally through Cuba, forcibly resettling perhaps 500 to 1,000 African-born slaves in the lower Brazos River valley. The males among those native Africans eventually became part of the Freedmen's Bureau's voter registration drive.[6] By 1870, six counties of the lower Brazos contained 16 percent of the state's African Americans. The region also claimed the horrible statistic of 32 percent of all of the known Black people murdered in the state between 1865 and 1868.[7]

It makes sense that racial conflicts took place in the areas in which Black people lived, although they did not necessarily occur where African Americans were in the majority. Most of the post-emancipation discord in Texas happened in counties where about one-third of the population was Black. And the struggle involved not just whether Black people would rise but which of the white factions would dominate. The squabbling over information began fairly soon after the war and reached its crescendo as Radicals escalated their investigation into violence as they came to power.[8]

The evolution of Texas placed within its borders people who became political adversaries over slavery and secession as the sectional crisis advanced. Migration to Texas exploded during the antebellum period in what one scholar has called a land rush.[9] The population grew from 142,000 in 1847 to 604,215 in 1860, with enslaved African Americans a little more than 30 percent of the final total. Although not a perfect description, people from the Lower South tended to settle in East Texas, while denizens from the Upper South chose the area around Austin, as well as North Texas. Unionism was strong in a half dozen or so counties toward the present-day Oklahoma border, with much of the in-migration occurring just before the Civil War. Virtually all of the slaveholdings lay east of the 98th meridian and served as a center of Black persecution after the war.[10]

Although Mexican-born Texans (Tejanos) play a significant role in the history of the state, they factored little in the story of the

Records Relating to Murders and Outrages. Tejanos had been force-fully absorbed as the region emerged as an independent republic in 1836. They lived mostly in South Texas toward the Rio Grande, where they encountered persecution from the largely Protestant Anglo majority because of their Catholic faith, their supposedly darker skin, and their antipathy for slavery.[11] Their diminished presence in the Freedmen's Bureau record was not because the war changed racial attitudes; they simply lived outside of the counties monitored by the bureau officers. Mexicans appeared within the Freedmen's Bureau record, but rarely. Yet they became scapegoats for conservatives during Reconstruction who attempted to explain away postwar atrocities as ethnic conflicts rather than political struggles.

Newer German immigrants became part of a Unionist coalition. As in many parts of the United States, two migrations had come from the German states. Earlier arrivals settled in the eastern portion of Texas and adopted Southern values. The more recent migration came after the Revolutions of 1848 throughout Europe, beaten down by a brutal counterreaction. The persecution chased to Texas the Forty-Eighters, who settled on the western edge of the state, espe-cially in Mason, Kerr, and Medina Counties.[12] Some came armed with revolutionary ideals, but they all espoused more democratic governance. And some had the audacity to express their opposition to slavery.[13]

Suspicions fell upon Germans, Mexicans, and recent immi-grants from the Upper South and the North for encouraging slave unrest. The three-month run of violence in 1860 known as the "Texas Troubles" intended to put down a suspected slave insur-rection. In July fires broke out in North Texas. The more paranoid slaveholders asserted that arsonists had set the fires to destroy arms in order to help a slave insurrection. Dozens of killings occurred, with hundreds more people whipped, beaten, and driven from communities.[14]

The fears were probably baseless, but the reaction demonstrated how easily Texans resorted to extralegal forms of justice. Historians have noted that using vigilance committees rather than courts to han-dle law and punishment was a national practice. While stronger in the South than in the North, the tendency was strongest yet in Texas, which experienced, according to one scholar's estimate, "no fewer than fifty-two vigilante movements in the nineteenth century."[15]

The sectional crisis drew hard lines between Unionists and secessionists that endured for the next decade. Sam Houston returned to the governor's office in 1859 as leader of the Unionists, whose cause was lost as secession fever gripped much of the Lower South. Although the support in Texas for joining the Confederacy was overwhelming, the debate over secession exposed that a stubborn group of Unionists existed, with die-hard Confederates determined not to let the spirit survive.[16]

During the war, Confederate residents harassed suspected enemies from within through the customary practice of extralegal justice.[17] Matters came to a head in 1862 as Confederate leaders and local militia moved to break resistance by Unionists to various government policies, especially conscription. Militia tracked down and arrested as many as 200 suspected Unionists in Cooke County near present-day Oklahoma. Arrests began on October 1, 1862, with 300 to 400 armed men collecting seventy prisoners. A so-called Citizens Court at the county seat of Gainesville charged the captives with treason and encouraging insurrection. The victims were hanged in various groupings over time, with eventually forty-one lynched and another two shot as they tried to escape.[18]

The persecution of Unionists in general created a steady stream of refugees. One historian has concluded that thousands passed through the northern border region of Mexico, with the majority trying to find their way back to the United States. Many arrived destitute with no extra clothing or money. Refugees recounted horror stories of comrades being arrested, hanged, or pressed into Confederate service.[19] Northern Texas also sustained a bleeding of settlers hoping to find more peaceful lives. By May 1861, an observer recorded that refugees clogged the road from Texas and Arkansas heading toward Kansas. The out-migration continued periodically. In the spring of 1864, Texas Rangers checking on the state's western defenses learned that several hundred families had given up and formed a wagon train to California.[20]

Unionist refugees also made their way to New Orleans, with some of the expatriates becoming significant players in the postwar battles for power in Texas. Exiled men included Brig. Gen. Andrew Jackson Hamilton, who became the provisional governor of Texas appointed by Johnson; Thomas H. Duval, a federal judge; and a federal customs agent. Most of the refugees, however, were laborers, farmers, or artisans. Traveling through Monterrey and Matamoros, these émigrés attempted to resume their lives back home after the conflict, which brought them face to face with secessionists who dealt harshly with the people they considered traitors to the Southern cause and to white society.[21]

These factions remained in place after the war with the balance of power in flux. Where they had been a minority, Unionists after Appomattox stood to gain a significant number of allies. Black people, Germans, and Hispanics had composed 37 percent of the 1860 Texas population. The freedpeople made up the largest portion of this bloc. If the men in these groups joined with white Unionists in a political party, it meant preventing secessionists from dictating state matters. This had repercussions for labor arrangements as well as race relations. And while the customary habits of extralegal violence continued, its location and targets changed. Lawlessness from desperadoes continued around the edges of the state— especially among white combatants in the north—but emancipation shifted the main battleground toward the plantation areas, which the Freedmen's Bureau duly noted in its monthly reporting.[22]

Peace did not come easily to portions of Texas. Civil and military authority collapsed with the surrender of Edmund Kirby Smith's Confederate forces in late May. Unpaid for a year, soldiers deserted the ranks even before the surrender. They looted the treasury and overran the government commissary for what they considered payment for services rendered. In some cases, Black and white civilians joined in the plundering of cities and towns. It took a few weeks for federal soldiers to establish a semblance of control. When they did, a federal general at Galveston announced on June 19, 1865, that all the enslaved people were free. Clashes continued between Unionists and secessionists in what some historians of the state have referred to as a Second Civil War.[23]

For the first year of occupation, the U.S. military stretched to meet divided priorities, limiting its ability to police white lawlessness. The French in Mexico caused the United States to station a majority of available troops at the Rio Grande to discourage encroachment by a monarchy. Disorder continued in Northeast Texas as ruthless men slipped between Missouri, Arkansas, Louisiana, and the Indian nations to commit crimes. The Red River region was particularly bloody. Civil authorities could not maintain law and order as perhaps a hundred gunmen terrorized the region. These battles featured old scores between white people and overlapped with changes in racial relations. Black people were targeted and killed, but of the thirty-three incident reports logged by Freedmen's Bureau officials for Grayson County in 1867, nearly a third involved white victims.[24]

It took until September 1865 for the Freedmen's Bureau to establish its headquarters in a customhouse in Galveston. At its height, the bureau grew to fifty-nine subagents and ten assistant subcommissioners—not enough to cover a vast region, although its agents did not have to police the entire state. Only a smattering of African Americans lived north of Waco on the Brazos River or north of Austin on the Colorado. Contributing to their difficulties in gathering intelligence on conflicts was that Freedmen's Bureau agents and officers experienced constant derision and intense resistance from former Confederates.[25]

In the summer of 1865, General Hamilton returned from exile in New Orleans to serve as provisional governor of Texas, which added fuel to the fire. He was a known Unionist who held animosity toward Confederate Texans, and his policies sparked an uptick in violence. The new governor used a heavy hand to ensure that only loyal men held public office, appointing Unionists to the positions of attorney general, comptroller, secretary of state, and district judges. Old allegiances fashioned during secession and war defined the political sides.

Gaining intelligence on violence represented a priority from the start, both for the new state regime and for federal officials. Information was particularly scarce in Texas because of its isolation during the war from Northern observers. Authorities sent Union officers into the state on fact-finding missions.[26] Reports made their way back to the governor that persecution continued against white Unionists and freedpeople, with public officials identifying the episodes as a power struggle between former masters and the freedpeople, often triggered by labor disputes. Governor Hamilton reported to President Johnson on July 24, 1865, that shooting and hanging of African Americans occurred "by the half dozens at a time, for the crime of leaving their former masters." The situation required more precise knowledge, prompting the War Department to investigate further. In January 1866 a military officer confirmed that there existed a "fearful state of things," believing that Texas featured more brutality than other states. He thought the army needed to sweep through the eastern portion, as Gen. William T. Sherman had done through South Carolina.[27]

In the turbulent times before Black suffrage, Confederate sympathizers held the upper hand in constructing new laws. The government organized in early 1866 featured a new state constitution that grudgingly acknowledged that force of arms had terminated slavery. In other words, the organic law of the state announced that the federal government had imposed emancipation on white Texans at the point of a gun. The constitution granted few concessions regarding the rights of freedpeople. Although Black men did not vote, they could testify in courts, but the wording left it up to judges and juries to determine the credibility of the testimony—meaning they could reject it. The constitution of 1866 also banned interracial marriages and public officeholding by African Americans. As for education, the document empowered the legislature to establish free public schools supported by a fund for white students only.[28]

Friction between state and federal authorities over the true nature of Reconstruction violence escalated with the incoming administration. Voters elected James W. Throckmorton, a Unionist who had voted against secession but had become a Confederate general during the war, as governor. He took office in August 1866 after defeating Elisha M. Pease, who had not supported the Confederacy. Both sides tried to define themselves as loyalists to the United States. Throckmorton's people called themselves Conservative Unionists, while Pease's followers designated themselves Radical Unionists, because they advocated better treatment of African Americans. Without Black voters to contend with, Throckmorton won handily.[29] Once in office, the new governor did little to stem the violence against Radical Unionists and Black people. Like many Southern white leaders, he did not give the reports of atrocities much credence.

Throckmorton, in fact, tried to confuse the situation by discounting the violence against Black people as far less important than the threat of Native Americans on the western fringes of Texas. Shortly after assuming office, the governor peppered the federal government with requests to shift troops to what he called the frontier to stave off alleged incursions by Comanches, Kiowas, and other tribes. Throckmorton and his allies believed they could control the Black population without military help and eyed a stable frontier as an imperative for future white settlement.

Sheridan and other military men considered the issue a pretext on the part of the governor that masked underlying reasons. They believed Throckmorton and his allies were trying to divert troops from the interior so that conservatives could continue the extralegal punishment of opponents and African Americans with less interference from the army. Sheridan told General Grant that he was skeptical of the accuracy of the news about Indian hostilities on the Texas frontier: "[T]here is a great deal of Bunkum in the reports." Alleged massacres of white settlers received no verification from cavalry troops stationed nearby. Additionally, soldiers believed that some Texans wanted troops to be relocated because doing so would offer "a fat job for contractors" who supplied the army with horses, equipment, and food. Moving the soldiers was also good for local business. Grant communicated his own doubts of the situation while forwarding these reports to President Johnson. He did not believe that diverting troops to the frontier would satisfy the situation. "Occasional murders will take place on our frontier," the general wrote, "and would if our people were all soldiers."[30]

The governor had exaggerated the situation. Some Native Americans had crossed over from Indian Territory, but they had not yet conducted extensive operations. In fact, it did not escape notice that former rebels killed more white and Black people than Indians did. Sheridan noted the irony to Throckmorton, writing that more casualties occurred "from outrages perpetrated upon Union men and freedmen in the interior of the state than occur from Indian depredations on the frontier." He also stated that the white public showed more excitement over a white man killed by an Indian than over a U.S. soldier killed by a rebel.[31] Sympathetic Northerners noticed the phenomenon, too. A Cincinnati newspaper observed in late 1866, "Eight or ten white men have been murdered on the frontier by Indians, whereupon Governor Throckmorton instituted a lengthy correspondence with General Sheridan, on the subject of raising volunteer troops or militia with which to repress such outrages. At the same time the killing, whipping, and cheating of freedmen progressed under his very nose almost, and not a word even of regret escaped his lips or pen."[32]

For the military charged with securing Texas, the priority for peacekeeping lay toward the settled regions of the interior—specifically the plantation areas in which Black people lived. Here officers and Freedmen's Bureau agents knew that violence reigned often unchecked, with far greater bloodshed than in the frontier to the west of Austin.

The conflict with the governor, however, further hampered a crackdown on violence as he caused the military to spread its limited resources. Throckmorton's persistent lobbying had an effect. President Johnson remained as sympathetic with Southern white ambitions as ever and blind to the atrocities committed against Black people. And he continued as commander in chief of the military. As the political pressure built, the army eventually had to concede to the white hatred of Native Americans in Texas. In October 1866 Sheridan was forced to divert twenty-one companies of the Fourth and Sixth Cavalry to the frontier. The action further diluted resources for protecting law and order in the heart of the state. The immense size of Texas—as well as political considerations for cutting the army's overall manpower—worked against establishing an effective police power.[33]

This brings us full circle to Henry Wilson, who in February 1867 read to his colleagues in the Senate an account of the outrages committed in the South. Although Wilson gave a sense of the horrors committed across the former Confederacy, the senator singled out Texas as a special illustration of the crimes against freedpeople. The state's unstable condition was hardly a secret. Even Johnson had omitted Texas from his April 1866 proclamation that declared the insurrection had ended. In August 1866, with the new government under Throckmorton, Johnson finally recognized Texas as restored. Yet the brutality in the state contradicted the president's position that a republican government functioned for all of its citizens.

The atrocities that Wilson shared with his colleagues and the public mirrored the terrorism employed throughout the South to maintain white supremacy. Assailants often came at night to surprise victims at their most vulnerable. As usual, women appeared in the record, although they were in the minority. Two had been taken from homes and raped, with one of them subsequently slain. The incident reports came from the places one might expect—Grayson and Fannin Counties up on the northern border, a handful of counties in the southeast near Houston, and a couple from near the state capital of Austin. Few of the crimes resulted in convictions. The last item on Wilson's list, for instance, mentioned a man found dead who had been tied, gagged, and shot, presumably by an employer. The assistant commissioner for the state indicated that he had little hope of resolving this or any of the other crimes. "Before the civil authorities of Texas," he wrote, "where a negro is the victim, acquittal follows murder as a matter of course."[34]

The violent conditions within Texas finally caught up with Throckmorton. In July 1867, as the Third Reconstruction Act clarified the military's authority over civil affairs, Sheridan removed the governor from office, beginning a purge that shifted political power in the state to Unionists who supported the Republican Party. Sheridan installed as governor Elisha M. Pease, who had run unsuccessfully against Throckmorton and whom many secessionists detested as a traitor to the Confederate cause and to his race. The removal of the entire executive department followed, as well as a reduction in the number of conservatives in public positions, including county offices. On November 1, 1867, a special order by the military commander removed roughly 400 conservatives from state and local posts. They were replaced by men deemed to be loyal, which meant they had been political enemies of the Confederate Texans. With suffrage coming for Black men, Republicans began to build a biracial political coalition.[35]

No matter how great the purge of officeholders, a large number of secessionists remained entrenched. The army simply could not find enough loyal people to replace them, which meant local law enforcement at times might still be hostile toward white and Black Republicans. And as the military commander of the state took steps intended to shore up law and order, it provoked more anger on the part of secessionists. In April 1867, Gen. Charles C. Griffin issued a "jury order" that allowed men to serve only if they could swear to the ironclad oath of 1862—meaning that jurors could not have aided the Confederacy in any way. Black men could sit in judgment on cases when ex-Confederates could not. The order added to the furor of former rebels.[36]

The reactionary movement rose with a vengeance in the summer of 1867 during the traditional opening of election season. Union Leagues organized Black people into Republican clubs to mobilize them for voting. Historians who have closely looked at the statistics in the murders and outrages reports have observed a correlation between rising violence and the Republican efforts to enfranchise Black men. Historian Barry A. Crouch noted that the number of Black people slain by whites rose twofold from 1866 to 1867 when freedmen won the right to vote. He added that 69 percent of all the Black people murdered by white people in these records took place between 1867 and 1868. Crouch concluded that "violence, terror, and intimidation became acceptable standards for the destruction of Black political equality."[37]

Random violence unrelated to elections certainly happened, but the examples of political assaults were hard to ignore. Voter registration, particularly of Black men, along with exclusion of disloyal former Confederates, intensified discord. In areas undergoing registration of voters, Freedmen's Bureau officials reported conflicts. In Northeast Texas, white people broke up religious gatherings as sites of voter mobilization. White people also shot at registrars in Washington County, while in other places planters fired freedmen from employment because of their political activity.[38]

The year ended with a disturbance during a Republican political meeting at Marshall in Harrison County, a community east of Dallas near Shreveport, Louisiana. On December 30, 1867, a justice on the Texas Supreme Court addressed a crowd of about 300 persons regarding the candidates for the coming constitutional convention. A snowstorm caused participants to meet in the basement of the courthouse. Judge Colbert C. Caldwell, a leading Republican, said that when a Black man accompanying him began to sing "Rally 'round the Flag, Boys" (also known as the Northern anthem "Battle Cry of Freedom"), "the tornado broke loose." A chief of police broke into the basement and fired a shot into the ceiling. The gesture intended to disperse the meeting, which succeeded. Caldwell wrote that the police chief, with others, pointed pistols directly at him and ordered the judge out of town or else he would be killed. He sought sanctuary with the U.S. military and from then on traveled with a soldier as a bodyguard.[39]

Minor in terms of loss of life, the incident not only captured the political tensions in Texas but also exposed the unhappiness of Radicals with the new military officer in charge of the state. They disagreed over the credibility of the information describing civil disorder. Pease and other state officials accused Gen. Winfield Scott Hancock of downplaying the violence. He was a known Democrat—a conservative unsympathetic to Black advancement and a subscriber to the president's views on Reconstruction. Reversing the trend of his predecessors, Hancock had assigned Democrats to public office. Shortly after assuming his post, he also issued General Orders No. 40 on November 29, 1867, which required his officers to take a back seat to local officials in the administration of justice. He considered the region at peace, as the president had declared, and that no grounds existed for the military to meddle with law and order.

To Radicals, nothing could have been further from the truth. General Orders No. 40 became a hated declaration that exposed them and their supporters to continued violence from rivals without threat of arrests by civil authorities or action by the army. The order caused Texas Republicans to turn to the records of the Freedmen's Bureau as they also launched their own investigation to prove Hancock wrong about the violence in the state and to lay blame for unrest on the general's negligence.

Arguments between Hancock and Peace over the reality of terrorism played out in the public record that captured Northern attention. Pease communicated his complaints to the U.S. Congress early in the new year as he looked to the creation of another constitutional convention to bring the state in line with the requirements for reinstatement in the Union. The attack on Judge Caldwell had distressed the governor. He feared that the cautious position by Hancock encouraged intimidation of voters that might jeopardize moving forward with a convention. He already knew of areas in the state where ex-Confederates refused to allow freedmen to vote. The governor bolstered his concerns with documents that laid out the assault on the political meeting led by Judge Caldwell, including an account from the judge himself. He added a clipping from an opposition newspaper to show its frightful spin on the incident. The *Marshall Republican*, as expected, characterized the affair as a mockery of justice. It proclaimed the fears of Caldwell groundless. And it argued that the testimony would not stand the test of judicial analysis. The item accused the judge of trying to capitalize politically on Black discontent, stirring up bad feelings in a time when the economy had ruined white farmers and forced them to lay off African American workers.[40]

The governor and the general also had clashed over the need for the military to take a firmer hand in ensuring justice for the murder of loyal men. Pease demanded a military commission to prosecute a homicide in Uvalde County. He feared—correctly as it turned out—that no justice would occur in this sparsely settled area near the frontier and that only the military could ensure law and order. Hancock refused, turning the suspect over to civil authorities, who let the man go. The general declined to order what he considered an imposition in civil affairs, adding that he believed the state was in a condition "of profound peace." This three-word phrase rankled the governor and his supporters, who argued that former rebels only grudgingly gave allegiance to the United States and that no fairness existed in civil tribunals. For the governor, war—not peace—represented the condition of the state. He went further by alleging that Hancock's loose supervision of civil matters had encouraged an escalation in outrages.[41]

Pease also launched a battle of numbers that hit a nerve. The governor stated, "It is a lamentable fact that over one hundred cases of homicide have occurred in Texas within the last twelve months, while not one-tenth of the perpetrators have even been arrested; and less than one-twentieth of them have been tried." He added that officers and soldiers of the United States had been killed doing their duty without the perpetrators tried or punished for the acts. Pease also claimed that grand juries failed to hand down indictments and that arrests were impossible because a majority of white citizens supported the outrages. He closed his letter with allegations that an increase in crime and hostile feelings toward the government could be traced to the November 29 order of Hancock and that appeals to the general for help had been ignored. In sum, the governor accused Hancock of allowing terrorism against Radicals to thrive.[42]

With his letter to Congress, Pease included an accounting of murders and assaults with intent to kill that had been committed in the state. The record tallied 411 incident reports, all of them for the year 1867. The information came partly from returns from the reports of the sub-assistant commissioners of the Freedmen's Bureau. Another enclosure contained 78 atrocities committed since Hancock had assumed command. These cases trickled over into early 1868 and had been assembled to prove the general's dereliction of duty. Spot-checking the material verifies that some of it, but not all, came from the record of criminal offenses committed from September

1865 through December 1868 that appears on the National Archives microfilm for the state of Texas. State officials like Pease used the Freedmen's Bureau to support their contentions about lawlessness, although not all of the atrocities involved acts against freedpeople or white Radicals.[43]

Hancock waited to mount a defense in a public letter written in early March 1868, as he was about to leave his post for another assignment. The general vigorously disputed Pease's claims. Hancock repeated the governor's description that large portions of the white population were embittered against the government, considered the Reconstruction legislation unconstitutional, and looked upon emancipation and disenfranchisement of their own class as an act of oppression. These were sentiments and emotions, not acts, causing Hancock to accuse the governor of failing to furnish evidence of malicious conflicts. "And this is all you have," he remarked, "to pres ent for proof that war and not peace prevails in Texas." One did not bring down despotic power on a populace merely because of their opinions and feelings. As for the difficulty in enforcing the law— having sheriffs who failed to do their duty and jurors who acquitted the guilty—Hancock echoed arguments that Democratic congress-men had raised while fighting passage of Military Reconstruction: "There is not a State in the Union, North or South, where the like facts are not continually happening." The problems were common everywhere.[44]

Hancock denied that there had been an increase in crime because of his stance against reviving military commissions. First of all, there could hardly be a causal relationship between General Orders No. 40 and the 100 murders Pease cited, for most of them came before the general assumed command. He conceded that the governor may have correct information, yet he tried to discredit the source while denying the conflicts were politically motivated. Native Americans and Mexicans proved to be convenient scapegoats. "The Freedmen's Bureau in Texas reported 160 [homicides]; how many of these were by Indians and Mexicans, and how the remainder were clas-sified, is not known; nor is it known whether these data are accu-rate." He then said that he had known of only eighteen homicides.

"Of these, five were committed by Indians; one by a Mexican; one by an insane man; three by colored men; two women by their husbands; and of the remainder, some by parties unknown." If a greater problem existed, Hancock wrote, then Pease deserved the blame, since he had the backing of the national government and the military had installed Radicals in public offices, including the judiciary. They were the ones who were negligent, maintained Hancock, not the army.[45]

The dispute enjoyed wide circulation in both North and South, partly because it provided Democrats with a defense of Johnson's position on Reconstruction as momentum built toward his impeachment trial. When the conflict first surfaced in January 1868, the *Tri-Weekly State Gazette* in Austin called the desire for martial law "a pretended necessity," adding, "The object was to get Congress to overthrow all [of] the reconstruction, designed by Lincoln and carried out by Johnson, and so arrange things that they might get office in spite of the people of Texas." General Hancock, in this view, saw through the subterfuge that Union men were in such grave danger that even Radical judges and juries could not be trusted to enact justice. After seeing Hancock's letter in March, the *Daily National Intelligencer, New York Herald*, and *Boston Post* all applauded the general's wisdom and reasoning. And the *New York World* accused Pease of lying about violence so the military would continue to prop up the Radical Party and stated that Hancock's letter offset "any number of lying 'specials'" to Radical journals about the situation in Texas.[46]

Matters did not rest there. The controversy stimulated an investigation by Republicans in Texas to prove that lawlessness had reached extraordinary proportions and that they needed stronger measures to protect citizens loyal to the government. In July 1868, a letter went from the president of the constitutional convention in Texas to the U.S. Congress that contained the results of the Special Committee on Lawlessness and Violence in Texas. This committee had been among the first organized as the delegates convened on June 1, which underscored the priority that battling the atrocities held. State lawmakers had grown desperate to curtail the outrages and argued for the creation of a state constabulary to combat the problem.[47]

TABLE 5.1. HOMICIDES IN TEXAS, 1865–1868

Year	Whites	Freedmen	Total
1865	47	51	98
1866	75	95	170
1867	173	174	347
1868	182	137	319
Year unknown	32	29	61
Race unknown			40
TOTAL	509	486	1,035

Source: Journal of the Reconstruction Convention, Which Met at Austin, Texas, June 1, A.D., 1868, 2 vols. (Austin: Tracy, Siemering, 1870), 1:501.

The Freedmen's Bureau provided a foundation for building this report, furnishing information from about sixty counties. Committee members also sought material from district courts, as well as sworn statements from witnesses throughout the state. The introduction to the data admitted that the information was incomplete—most likely understated. The criminal activity gleaned by state officials from court records came from only forty counties. And the committee recognized that threats of assassination had stifled testimony. Nonetheless, the committee tried to present statistics that passed a test for veracity: cases officially reported by law enforcement or distinctly remembered by witnesses who testified under oath.[48]

The report concentrated on murders rather than outrages as it tallied the people killed from the close of the rebellion to June 1868. It noted that whites had killed 373 African Americans, while only 10 white people had been killed by freedpeople. A second, supplemental report upped the total murders to 1,035. Both reports revealed that more white people had been killed (509) than Black people (486), although the 40 victims whose racial background remained unknown may have closed or widened this gap (see table 5.1). One historian has calculated from these figures that 1 percent of all Black males between the ages of fifteen and forty-five died from violence in this four-year period. Meanwhile, the report claimed that a majority of the slain white people were Union men with assailants primarily former Confederates.[49]

Without using the term "political terrorism," the report left little doubt that it viewed much of the violence in that way. The white people who had participated in the rebellion, according to the committee, "are now intensely embittered against the freedmen on account of their emancipation and enfranchisement, and on account of their devotion to the republican party, and against the loyal whites for their persistent adhesion to the Union; . . . that it is their purpose even by desperate measures to create such a state of alarm and terror among Union men and freedmen as to compel them to abandon the advocacy of impartial suffrage or fly from the state." It added that "bad men do not fear the civil courts of Texas." Between 1865 and 1867, records contained 249 indictments for murder in district courts with only five convictions—or 2 percent of the total. Out of the roughly 1,000 murders committed, only one had resulted in an execution.[50]

As further proof that terrorists targeted white Unionists, the committee gave examples of Republicans persecuted because of their political positions. A "rebel" killed a judge in Uvalde County in 1867. Similarly, assassins had slain the son of a Union man appointed judge in Blanco County. Assailants gunned down the son while plowing in his field before his father assumed his place on the bench. This attempt to chase the judge from the county succeeded. In another case, four men were murdered in Hunt County and six in Bell County for their "loyalty." Additionally, rebels drove the county judge and the district clerk of Hunt County from their homes; they fled the region for their lives. The report said it was impossible to avoid the conclusion that Unionists were mowed down for their political beliefs. "In other words," the report concluded, "if they were rebels they would not be killed."[51]

Finally, the committee mustered evidence that General Hancock deserved blame for an increase in the violence, disputing the general's allegation that negligence by Republican officeholders had caused the situation. The committee pointed out that it was not true that Radicals held a majority of state offices. Of 1,975 elective offices in Texas, according to the report, only 402 had been appointed by the military. Some of the appointees had refused to serve because of threats of assassination, "in which cases the old incumbents continue to act." The report estimated that only about a fifth of the officers in Texas could be relied on to be loyal. In the meantime, lawlessness continued largely because, according to the committee, Hancock had entrusted law and order to the very people who encouraged the outrages.[52]

Remarkably, the crime statistics released by the committee were generally accepted as valid by delegates at the convention on both sides of the aisle. Representatives shared a concern over the rising frequency of crime, but they differed on the reasons. Where Radical Unionists saw assaults aimed at loyal people, conservatives believed that a lack of strong government allowed for the outrages. They could not deny that violence happened—too much evidence existed to the contrary. Yet opponents vehemently denied the accusations that a majority of the murders and physical assaults contained a political intent.[53]

One such man, W. H. Mullins, told his fellow delegates that none of the public officials killed had been targeted on account of their loyalty, and he strongly claimed that no evidence existed that any one of them died for their Unionism. "These homicides have been committed without reference to party, race, or color, and the cause of them can justly be attributed to no other source than a want of an efficient, strong, civil government." The blame for that, he said, resided with Republicans. He believed that civil authorities had become befuddled over law enforcement, because the frequent changes made by Radicals had not allowed the newcomers time to learn their jobs. They lacked the experience to handle the tasks they faced. This represented a slight twist on Hancock's assertion that Republicans bore the responsibility for the violence because of their own negligence. And as for the murders of Republican judges and officials, well, Mullins attributed some of that simply to long-standing family feuds.[54]

While Texas was extraordinary in its scale of atrocities, it was unremarkable in repeating the pattern of violence found in Louisiana and Georgia from 1865 to 1868. After a brief lull at the start of Military Reconstruction in the spring of 1867—followed by an increase during voter registration later that year—persecution of Black people escalated during the elections for constitutional conventions. As in other parts of the South, the Klan made its presence felt. One historian, in fact, has upped the number of terrorist groups from earlier studies. Where Allen Trelease uncovered seventeen such groups, James Smallwood has placed their number at more than sixty, going by names such as the Ku Klux Klan, the Knights of the White Camellia, and the Teutonic Knights, to name a few. They operated in more than sixty counties, especially in East and Northeast Texas. The violence reached its peak in July and August 1868, corresponding with debates on civil rights in the constitutional convention and mobilization by Union Leagues.[55]

One of the larger confrontations of Klan violence over politics came in the small town of Millican in the Brazos River valley in July 1868. This incident stood out for the armed Black resistance and the subsequent slayings of the leaders. In early June, the Klan marched through the town and fired shots at African Americans holding what may have been a prayer meeting. In response, Pastor George Edwin Brooks—who had rallied Black people to chase off the Klan—mobilized a civilian force of about 200 African Americans. A Methodist preacher, Brooks had been a Union soldier and served as an organizer for the Union League. White people became anxious over the resistance. Nerves had frayed in a season of political campaigning for the constitutional convention that affirmed Republican control of the state.

On July 15, rumors flashed about the murder of a Black man. African American militia marched to investigate and met a force of white men raised by the sheriff. Gunfire broke out; it concluded quickly, but the situation did not end there. The mayor called for white men to rally, attracting a force ranging from 125 to 500 men. It took a couple of days for intervention by the military to calm matters. The estimates of the dead have varied widely: the Freedmen's Bureau listed perhaps 9 Black men killed; historians' figures have ranged from 25 to, more recently in a project at Texas A&M

University, a span of 5 to 150. The Klan tried to break the resistance of African Americans by attacking their leaders. Among the slain was Brooks, the Black pastor. Rebels hunted him down, captured him, and tortured him to death.[56]

Intimidation occurred in other parts of the state, too. During election of convention delegates, armed mobs had attacked polling places in Augustine County; in Bastrop, disorder caused election officials to suspend the balloting. Terrorists targeted Black men who served on the registry board, killing three during 1868 and firing upon and threatening others. Two sub-assistant commissioners of the Freedmen's Bureau also were slain. In June of that year, according to the bureau records, three unidentified men entered a home in Falls County, gunned down two freedmen, and shouted as they rode off that they had a hundred more men doing the same to Black men who belonged to the Loyal League. One historian has concluded that the attacks on the freedpeople to chill political participation during voting for a constitutional convention in February 1868 "were the most murderous, brutal and extensive of the entire 1867- 1868 period."[57]

Gen. J. J. Reynolds called civil law east of the Trinity River "almost a dead letter." He noted the prevalence of the Klan, indicating that members attended openly in large numbers the political barbecues conducted by Democrat clubs. During such meetings, Reynolds said, it was not unusual for speakers to call out the names of men selected for murder. He concluded that the official reports of lawlessness and crime, "so far from being exaggerated, do not tell the whole truth."[58]

A remarkable number of African Americans voted despite this intimidation. The February 1868 voting for the constitutional convention had resulted in 89 percent of registered Black people casting ballots, as opposed to 31 percent of registered white men. Texas was one of the three states not yet organized and thus ineligible for the presidential election in the fall. But when it came time to elect a governor in 1869, turnout by Black people remained vibrant despite efforts to dissuade them, at the cost of many lives. The fears of secessionists had become realized. A combination of white Unionists and Black people installed Edmund Davis in the governor's office. A Radical, Davis supported the rights of Black Texans. By 1870, the state had become reconstructed, and its legislature created the state police force that Pease had lobbied for during his tenure.[59]

In the meantime, the Freedmen's Bureau faded from the scene. Its agents had given way grudgingly in the face of ever-increasing restraints placed on them by General Hancock. Some ignored his orders and tried to hold courts instead of having civil authorities adjudicate cases involving the freedpeople. After Hancock stepped down in the spring of 1868, General Reynolds tried to have officers protect freedpeople. But it was a confusing time for the bureau, with contradictory policy positions, ever-increasing political pressure, and a clock ticking down its tenure. After December 1868, it was largely dismantled in Texas, although it continued to supervise education for a while longer.[60]

One of the underappreciated legacies of the bureau came in the creation of a paper trail that testified to the horrors confronting Black and white supporters of the Union. The record not only cataloged the atrocities but also became part of policy discussions in both national and state halls of lawmaking. It did not stem the violence, at least not in any way that can be measured. The belief in its accurate depiction of murders and outrages justified federal actions during Reconstruction. If the violence had been exaggerated for partisan reasons, then military rule truly was a tragedy. But if it was real, as historians now believe, then the invalidation of state governments, institution of Black suffrage, and adoption of key amendments to protect the rights of individuals from harm and from restrictions at the ballot box—all of this occurring through the power of the bayonet—was not only necessary but welcome.

EPILOGUE
PROVING LYNCHING

Racial violence outlasted the Freedmen's Bureau; so did the need to prove it happened. In the 1870s, the federal government sought African American testimony during congressional hearings on the dangers of the Ku Klux Klan. That effort contributed to the collapse of the first generation of the Klan, although Southern Democrats subsequently employed other terrorism to overturn Republican-led governments. Later in the century, however, Black people took the lead in revealing the atrocities they were suffering under the oppressions of Jim Crow America. Though lynching had been practiced since the antebellum era against all races across America, it transformed during the 1880s into violence targeting primarily Black males in the South. In the 1890s, African Americans turned to data collection both to demonstrate lynching's prevalence and to overturn a central mythology surrounding its causes.[1]

At the heart of this mission was Ida B. Wells-Barnett, whose anti-lynching pamphlets echoed efforts of Black politicians in 1868 to petition for federal intervention by using Freedmen's Bureau reports. Gathering data for the freedom struggle had even deeper roots, dating at least to the abolition movement of the 1830s, when activists combed thousands of Southern newspapers for runaway slave ads to reveal the brutality embedded in the slave system.[2] Wells-Barnett was influenced in her approach by investigative journalism and by the emergence of sociology as a tool for reform. She conducted her investigations nearly at the same time as W. E. B. Du Bois, the first African American to earn a doctorate from Harvard, who employed similar methodology for proving discrimination against urban Black people, publishing his research in 1899 in *The Philadelphia Negro*.[3] Wells-Barnett similarly used case studies and numbers to convince a white mainstream that change had to come.

A Red Record: Tabulated Statistics and Alleged Causes of Lynching in the United States (1895) contained the numbers, identities, and alleged crimes of the victims of lynching in the United States, especially for the year 1893. In those twelve months, Wells-Barnett tallied 200 lynchings throughout the country; most of the victims were Black men lynched in the states of the former Confederacy. She organized her tabulation under the crimes that white people alleged had justified the torture, burning, and hanging of Black people in public. In so doing, Wells-Barnett combated the widely repeated notion that lynching was the justifiable murder of Black men for raping white women. Her statistics demonstrated that murder, not rape, served as a leading charge against Black lynching victims—a fact consistent across many years. Even when the charge of rape exceeded that of murder in a particular year, alleged sexual assaults constituted only about a third of the total incidents. However, she and other African Americans understood that the "crimes" themselves were typically false, manufactured by white supremacists as an excuse for the violent repression of Black independence.[4]

Wells-Barnett's *Red Record* relied heavily on information gathered and published by the *Chicago Tribune*, which had been a Radical Republican newspaper during the Civil War and Reconstruction. In those years, critics routinely argued that African American testimony of outrages were exaggerated. The same held true later in the century. So Wells-Barnett's *Red Record* used "the statistics as gathered and preserved by white men" because they had "not been questioned." She added, "Out of their own mouths shall the murderers be condemned."[5]

Beginning with atrocities occurring during 1882, the *Chicago Tribune* published an annual accounting of lynchings. At first, the information was published under the headline "Necrology," which recalled the famous artists, clergymen, politicians, and business leaders who had passed in the previous year.[6] Over time, however, lynching became more prominent in the compilation, with the newspaper distinguishing between the work of "Jack Ketch" (state-sanctioned executions by hanging) and that of "Judge Lynch" (extralegal executions). The statistics for 1883 noted that 190 people had been lynched, though white victims outnumbered Black. The largest state total involved 40 people in Montana, executed allegedly for cattle and horse rustling. By the mid-1880s, however, the number of Black people slain in this fashion outnumbered white people, a trend that continued well into the twentieth century.[7]

Comparative statistics need to be dealt with carefully, because not enough is known about lynching before 1882. Analysis of the crime during Reconstruction remains an emerging area of study. One exception has been work on violence in Louisiana, which documented 124 Black and 46 white deaths from lynching between 1866 and 1876. The Equal Justice Initiative in Montgomery, Alabama, also has expanded its efforts to trace lynching's roots by digging into the Reconstruction era. Its early efforts have led to an estimate of at least 2,000 Black victims lynched from 1865 to 1876, with evidence painstakingly combed from a combination of the Freedmen's Bureau's reports, other government records, and newspaper accounts. The estimate remains imperfect, with the investigators arguing that the numbers are almost surely higher, given many undocumented lynchings that have been lost to history.[8]

To her credit, Wells-Barnett dated the emergence of lynching against African Americans to emancipation, but at the time she had little supporting data to back her conclusion. The Freedmen's Bureau reports that could have aided her efforts were not well known. Wells-Barnett's correspondence in the early 1890s showed she had little knowledge of the evidence that the agency left behind as she hunted statistics on violence from Reconstruction. She was not alone. Few people at the time grasped the nature of the bureau's records, a situation lamented in 1912 by a professional historian who wrote about the unexplored treasures lying unused in the National

Archives. Even if Wells-Barnett had known about the material, the archives' volume of roughly 1,000 cubic feet, the lack of finding aids, and the limited access to the archives prevented easy use. Into the twenty-first century the records of the Freedmen's Bureau remain difficult to use, a fact noted in a 2000 congressional hearing that argued for improved preservation and access through microfilming to encourage wider use of the collection, including by genealogists.[9]

In any case, it seems certain that a majority of lynchings occurred in the South in the late nineteenth century. Wells-Barnett's data attested to this regional prevalence, and Northern newspapers like the *Chicago Tribune* increasingly condemned the atrocity as a Southern, sectional phenomenon aimed at African Americans. One headline proclaimed, "Judge Lynch's Work: The Large Majority of His Victims Is in the South." Referencing events in 1893, the same year that Wells-Barnett had highlighted in her *Red Record*, the story noted that occurrences had fallen slightly because of Northern practices but added, "In the South, it is the old, old story." The condemnation of the violence as a sectional practice escalated in the decade before the turn of the century.[10]

The *New York Herald* joined the outcry against lynching, reinforcing how common it had become for activists to use statistics to underscore the extent of the horror. The newspaper printed a long column from rival editor T. Thomas Fortune, whose *New York Age* was a leading voice for Black America. Fortune, as the headline indicated, quoted "Some Astounding Figures" that showed the pervasiveness of lynching. He castigated the surrender by Northerners that had allowed the white South to reestablish "home rule" and white supremacy through violence. Many Northerners had overlooked this strategy, he maintained, because they took Southern whites at their word that they would govern peacefully. That trust had been betrayed. To prove his point, he cited the number of people lynched for each year between 1882 and 1892. All told, according to Fortune, 728 Black people had suffered death at the hands of Judge Lynch.[11]

Fortune borrowed his data from Wells-Barnett, which was no coincidence. In 1892, she had fled her native Memphis, Tennessee, after writing an editorial for the *Memphis Free Speech* that condemned the lynching of three acquaintances. The incident had ignited her activism. Reestablishing herself in New York, she became co-owner of the *New York Age* with Fortune and produced *Southern Horrors*, whose statistics on lynching had appeared previously in the newspaper on June 25, 1892. She and other Black activists compiled and disseminated evidence to awaken the nation to the racial crimes that white people committed under false pretenses.[12]

They used the information to lobby for legislative change. Two years before she published *A Red Record*, Wells-Barnett attended a convention of Black men in Cincinnati that proposed a national council to report on persons murdered by mobs. A newspaper report on the convention concluded, "The Southern papers and the Southern men who have tried to excuse the white males, by the general charge that all negroes lynched have been guilty of one of the most fiendish crimes on record, can no longer deal in generalities." The next step, the report noted, was to advocate for laws allowing the prosecution of those who conducted lynchings.[13]

Wells-Barnett was not alone in using case studies and statistics in the hopes that truth-telling might result in justice. In 1901, John Edward Bruce published a treatise that echoed the title of Wells-Barnett's pamphlet. *Blood Red Record* opened with a story from an unidentified newspaper published in New York City about people burned at the stake for alleged crimes. Bruce also tapped the *Chicago Tribune* for data on lynching. Yet another important information source was created by Monroe N. Work, who began including statistics in the *Negro Year Book*, which debuted in 1912. Hired by Booker T. Washington, Work served as director of records and research for the Tuskegee Institute. He earned a national reputation as one of the most influential compilers of lynching statistics, superseding the *Chicago Tribune* as a resource for a generation of scholars and public activists.[14]

Had a former Freedmen's Bureau agent been around to analyze the lynching statistics, he would have seen only small changes from his own time in the geographic distribution of violence. As during Reconstruction, the Deep South dominated in frequency of cases, but in the 1890s a few states came to the fore that had been in the background. Alabama and Arkansas made stronger appearances, often topping the lists of annual lynchings. Mississippi also often counted among the leaders. These states were underrepresented in the Records Relating to Murders and Outrages, although this owed to the idiosyncratic way the data were compiled. Additionally, Texas started out among the leading states for lynchings but then, according to the statistics of the *Chicago Tribune*, declined in comparison with other states in the Deep South. Violence against Black people had not ebbed there, however. A recent study of Texas indicated that even as lynching faded in frequency, mob violence remained endemic for African Americans in the Lone Star State.[15]

The *Chicago Tribune* neglected to say how it compiled the information, making it difficult to evaluate the thoroughness of its efforts and how it compared with the bureau's. The newspaper could not have amassed the data in quite the same way as the Freedmen's Bureau since it did not have agents stationed in localities throughout the killing zones. The presence of the federal government during Reconstruction—as imperfect as it was for recording atrocities and protecting lives—increased the chances for Black people to make their way to officials to report injustice. The *Tribune*, which reported on lynching consistently throughout the year, likely used clipping and wire services to prepare the record, with perhaps some testimony from African American witnesses. How much and in what ways remain unknown. The compilation did not originate with the government—a key difference from the earlier era—which limited the impact of the record gathering and lobbying in the anti-lynching campaign.

During Reconstruction, Congress and portions of the executive branch were comparatively more sympathetic about controlling violence in the South. The Freedmen's Bureau collected information on atrocities through the efforts of African Americans because Republicans wanted to justify martial law. Additionally, public officials and military leaders like Ulysses S. Grant supported the campaign to prove Southern white intransigence. Although we should not assume that Northerners did so only from altruistic motives, the political will existed to try to curb the atrocities, along with a desire to punish the rebels who seemed reluctant to concede that they had lost the war.

To some extent, the violence resulting from Presidential Reconstruction backfired at first on Southern whites as it provided greater impetus for moderates in the North to support Radical measures to disband Southern governments and institute new ones with Black male suffrage. The imperatives of national institutions and African Americans intersected, although both came to this point along different paths. Helping forge this dynamic was the military, in the form of the Freedmen's Bureau. Soldiers reported violent incidents, opening the country's eyes to the atrocities committed in the South. They became the record keepers who have made it possible to document and remember the violence against Black people. And they served at times almost like an investigative arm of the legislative branch. Their efforts contributed to the momentum for Black males to vote and serve in public office so they could represent their own interests and construct safeguards against the violence.

In contrast, the anti-lynching campaign lacked the backing of the federal government. African Americans in the later nineteenth century faced a society where the Supreme Court had diluted the promise of the Fourteenth Amendment and the Civil Rights Acts of 1866 and 1875, limiting the federal government's intervention in protecting individual rights. The Republican Party learned by the 1896 presidential election that it no longer needed Black votes in the South to win a national contest—one less reason to push for legislative safeguards at the federal level. Activists like Wells-Barnett and Fortune had to work hard just to gain the government's attention, much less compel it to act.

Anti-lynching activists in the late nineteenth century conducted their effort as racial studies in the sciences and humanities reinforced in the public mind a tendency to diminish reports of violence against Black people. The historians who emerged during the escalation in lynching prided themselves on empiricism, claiming that they based judgments upon careful examination of previously untapped sources such as government documents. They provided insights into high-level politics, constitutional issues, and legislation that remain useful starting points. But when it came to assessing the murders and outrages during Reconstruction, early scholarship ignored the testimony of African Americans. Instead, historians who mined congressional reports for information on freedpeople channeled the criticism of Democrats, dismissing bureau officers as ardent Unionists who hated the South and functioned as an arm of the Republican political machine.[16]

James Ford Rhodes, an industrialist from Ohio, made enough money to devote himself to the life of a gentleman historian. An important figure in the development of American history as a discreet field of study, Rhodes rejected the idea that lawlessness had necessitated Military Reconstruction. He specifically scorned Henry Wilson's account in the Senate of 375 murders and 556 outrages—information supplied by the Freedmen's Bureau. Rhodes stated, "The subject was approached by the Radicals with the desire to find facts to bolster up the policy which they had determined on rather than to get at the exact truth." He concluded, "Naturally the trouble was exaggerated."[17]

The denial continued in the wave of historical studies generated at Columbia University by what became called the Dunning school. Led by Professor William A. Dunning, seminars tackled various subjects of Reconstruction history, resulting in a collection of monographs that methodically studied the individual states of the former Confederacy and that influenced scholarly and public interpretation for much of the twentieth century. In general, they depicted Radical Reconstruction as a mistake, especially the institution of Black suffrage. Most of the volumes took the inferiority of African Americans for granted, judging them as ill-prepared to handle such a responsibility. They also tended to present a moderate portrayal of white treatment of freedpeople. John W. Burgess, one of the central figures in this school of thought and an influential colleague of Dunning, flat-out described talk of outrages as the "most extravagant tales."[18]

Members of the Dunning school used evidence from government reports selectively. Dunning himself looked at the 1866 report of the Freedmen's Bureau and claimed that its assessments of white treatment of Black people "were almost uniformly of a reassuring tone." Abuses of the freedpeople, he maintained, had declined, and state courts treated them fairly. Rhodes followed suit in using the same report to claim that careful analysis refused to support the contentions of widespread bloodshed. Both men based conclusions on limited portions of the documentary record; other sections detailed a litany of abuses that included banning Black people from bearing arms for personal defense, unrest by freedpeople in Virginia who threatened retaliation for injustice in civil courts, burning of Black churches, and shootings of Black people and reported rapes in North Carolina. Dunning and his colleagues also ignored assessments by military officers of the exceptional violence that raged in both Texas and Louisiana.[19]

Only in the 1960s did historians begin to accept reports of murders and outrages as credible and as a driving force behind intervention by the military. In 1962, John A. Carpenter chastened scholars for the equivocation that greeted the reports of atrocities. He saved his greatest exasperation for the first comprehensive study of the Freedmen's Bureau by George R. Bentley. Published in 1955, Bentley's *History of the Freedmen's Bureau* admitted that atrocities had happened, but the author added that bureau agents were prone to exaggerate the incidents and reported rumors without screening them for authenticity. Carpenter could not help but comment, using punctuation to signal his recognition of the ridiculous contradiction: "In one sentence he admits that there was 'considerable truth in the . . . reports' and in four pages he shows how such reports were exaggerated!"[20] Especially in the 1970s, the tide turned as historians began using the papers of the Freedmen's Bureau as a credible exposé of Southern atrocities.[21]

With the legal system, historical interpretation, and public attitudes stacked against African Americans until the middle of the twentieth century, it was no wonder that Wells-Barnett and her compatriots faced enormous odds in advocating for anti-lynching laws. Though they did not succeed in securing passage of federal anti-lynching legislation, they did achieve some change at the state level. Georgia and North Carolina adopted anti-lynching legislation in 1893, followed by Texas in 1892 and South Carolina in 1895.

These actions, however, hardly stopped the violence; as one historian noted, "Enforcement of these laws was at best sporadic."[22] Federal legislation repeatedly introduced over more than a century never had the backing to pass. In 2019, the House of Representatives finally passed legislation that recognizes lynching as a hate crime, although the bill, named for lynching victim Emmett Till, was, as of this writing, stalled in the Senate.[23]

One of the first steps toward reconciling wrongs in the past is recovering personal stories and trying to account for the dead. We make lists. We compile names. In these acts, we seek to overcome the past repression of these people's memory. Reconstruction-era Democrats and the Progressive Era historians who followed scoffed at the accounts produced by the freedpeople and the Freedmen's Bureau, documenting racial injustice in the post–Civil War South. Decrying accounts of violence as the overblown product of naysayers, unpatriotic citizens, demagogues, or revisionists, these powerful people buried evidence that is essential to a full reckoning of our nation's history.

Today, organizations like the Equal Justice Initiative have taken up the mantle of Ida B. Wells-Barnett, working again to document the thousands of incidents of racial terror committed in the United States. While addressing the contemporary atrocity of mass incarceration for African Americans, the Equal Justice Initiative's National Memorial for Peace and Justice has sought to reclaim the names and dates of all the African Americans killed through lynching—a total that now exceeds 4,400.[24]

We make lists. We compile names.

One way to measure the impact of people like Wells-Barnett and Fortune has been offered by scholars who see them as representative of a Black counter-public sphere that prevented atrocities from passing unnoticed. Journalists, editors, authors, intellectuals, and clubwomen put on record evidence that belied the denial of atrocities among the white majority. Historian Kidada Williams has said these Black activists pushed their way into the dominant public sphere, creating an alternative discourse to white supremacy. This offered neither justice nor reparations to victims, but it is significant to have a record of wrongdoing. It has left the possibility of an accounting. Williams acknowledged that the African Americans who conducted this struggle in the late nineteenth century carried on a legacy that reached back to pioneering efforts of Black leaders such as Frederick Douglass, Henry Highland Garnet, David Walker, and Maria Stewart.[25] We can add to this list the freedpeople like Cato Allums and countless thousands of others who made their way to Freedmen's Bureau agents to ensure that their stories were heard, recorded, and remembered.

ACKNOWLEDGMENTS

This project benefited enormously from the help of undergraduate and graduate students who spent time going through the microfilm reels of atrocities, building spreadsheets of incident reports, and tallying the kinds of violence committed in the post–Civil War South. I am grateful for the hard work of former students Brandon T. Benner and Corey Pittounicos, who spent portions of their junior and senior years wading through awful reports of violence to collect them on spreadsheets. Graduate students Tyler Sperrazza, Cecily Zander, and Megan Hildebrand Kessler performed invaluable help in counting incident reports, verifying tabulations, and combing congressional records. I look forward to seeing the results of their own exciting projects in the future.

Colleagues have helped me sharpen the ideas within this manuscript. I am grateful to Gary W. Gallagher, Steven Berry, Patrick Kelly, Deb Poveromo, and Hal Rosenberg for reading portions of the work and to Mark E. Neely Jr., and Nan Elizabeth Woodruff for wading through and commenting on the entire study. Nan's invaluable guidance prodded me to look for the connections of data collection between Reconstruction and lynching. To further the research, I benefited from a semester's funding by the Center for Humanities and Information at Penn State, which also placed me in contact with scholars interested in the creation of information. And I received insights from presenting what became chapter 2 and a portion of chapter 4 at the 2017 conference in State College sponsored by the Richards Civil War Era Center, "Rethinking Violence in African American History: History, Memory, Trauma." The feedback allowed me to identify additional sources and proceed more confidently in the analysis of the Bossier Parish massacre in Louisiana. I also want to thank the readers for the University of North Carolina Press and Mark Simpson-Vos, editorial director of the Press, whose wise guidance helped me get over the finish line.

Finally, I owe the greatest debt, as always, to Mary Ann Blair, who patiently dealt with my anxieties and sorrows in the course of researching and writing this book. I could not have made it without her.

NOTES

INTRODUCTION

1. Records of the Assistant Commissioner for the State of Virginia, reel 59, M1048, RG 105, Bureau of Refugees, Freedmen, and Abandoned Lands, National Archives (hereafter BRFAL, NA).

2. On the denial of the Klan's existence, see Elaine Frantz Parsons, "Klan Skepticism and Denial in Reconstruction-Era Public Discourse," *Journal of Southern History* 77 (February 2011): 53–90.

3. John William De Forest, *A Union Officer in the Reconstruction*, ed. James H. Croushore and David Morris Potter (1948; new ed., Baton Rouge: Louisiana State University Press, 1976), 1; A. P. Ketchum to Each Assistant Commissioner, September 24, 1866, image 227, reel 2, M742, RG 105 BRFAL, NA; John Y. Simon, ed., *The Papers of Ulysses S. Grant*, 32 vols. (Carbondale: Southern Illinois University Press, 1967–2012), 17:50n. Also see John A. Carpenter, *Sword and Olive Branch: Oliver Otis Howard* (Pittsburgh: University of Pittsburgh Press, 1964), 129.

4. Making a similar case for the influence of Black testimony is Kidada E. Williams, *They Left Great Marks on Me: African American Testimonies of Racial Violence from Emancipation to World War I* (New York: New York University Press, 2012).

5. An early exception among historians was W. E. B. Du Bois, *Black Reconstruction in America, 1860–1880*, with an introduction by David Levering Lewis (1935; repr., New York: Free Press, 1998). In the 1960s, John A. Carpenter singled out the work of George R. Bentley as he challenged the field to take seriously the violence collected by the Freedmen's Bureau. See Carpenter's "Atrocities in the Reconstruction Period," *Journal of Negro History* 47 (October

1962): 235–36. Bentley had continued to claim that reports of violence had been exaggerated in his *History of the Freedmen's Bureau* (Philadelphia: University of Pennsylvania Press, 1955). Besides journal literature in the 1960s, the monographs that featured a more sympathetic view of the Freedmen's Bureau's data were Allen W. Trelease, *White Terror: The Ku Klux Klan Conspiracy and Southern Reconstruction* (New York: Harper and Row, 1971); and George C. Rable, *But There Was No Peace: The Role of Violence in the Politics of Reconstruction* (Athens: University of Georgia Press, 1984). For the Freedmen's Bureau effort, see the Freedmen and Southern Society Project website, accessed January 17, 2020, www.freedmen.umd.edu; and The Freedmen's Bureau Online, accessed April 10, 2020, www.freedmensbureau.com/outrages.htm. The literature on violence during Reconstruction has become too extensive to list here. For recent examples, see Hannah Rosen, *Terror in the Heart of Freedom: Citizenship, Sexual Violence, and the Meaning of Race in the Postemancipation South* (Chapel Hill: University of North Carolina Press, 2009); Gregory P. Downs, *After Appomattox: Military Occupation and the Ends of War* (Cambridge, Mass.: Harvard University Press, 2015); Carole Emberton, *Beyond Redemption: Race, Violence, and the American South after the Civil War* (Chicago: University of Chicago Press, 2013); and Williams, *They Left Great Marks on Me*.

6. For an overview of the Freedmen's Bureau records and a breakdown of the state records on microfilm, see the web page African American Heritage on the National Archives and Record Administration website, accessed July 17, 2020, www.archives.gov/research/african-americans/freedmens-bureau. All of this is in the larger collection of RG 105, BFRAL, NA.

7. Du Bois saw a similar progression in terrorism as he analyzed reports by the Freedmen's Bureau and the Ku Klux Klan hearings. See his *Black Reconstruction in America*, 670.

8. Historians of Texas and Louisiana have produced some of the most penetrating looks at violence through mining the Records Relating to Murders and Outrages. For an overview of the Texas historiography, see Kenneth W. Howell, ed., *Still the Arena of Civil War: Violence and Turmoil in Reconstruction Texas, 1865–1874* (Denton: University of North Texas Press, 2012), introduction. On Louisiana, see Gilles Vandal, *Rethinking Southern Violence: Homicides in Post–Civil War Louisiana, 1866–1884* (Columbus: Ohio State University Press, 2000).

9. Eric Foner, "Why Reconstruction Matters," *New York Times*, March 28, 2015; Equal Justice Initiative, "Reconstruction in America: Racial Violence after the Civil War, 1865–1876," Equal Justice Initiative, accessed August 5, 2020, https://eji.org/reports/reconstruction-in-america-overview/. Also see James W. Loewen, "Five Myths about Reconstruction," *Washington Post*, January 21, 2016.

CHAPTER 1

1. *Cincinnati Daily Gazette*, February 23, 1867; *Flake's Weekly Galveston Bulletin*, March 6, 1867; *Washington (Pa.) Reporter*, March 6, 1867; *Freedom's Champion* (Atchison, Kans.), March 7, 1867; *San Antonio Express*, March 13, 1867; *National*

Aegis, March 9, 1867; *Congressional Globe*, 39th Cong., 2nd sess., 1375–76 (1867). The *Globe* dates this debate to February 15, but the newspapers concur that February 19 was the day.

2. *Congressional Globe*, 1441; on Sumner, see *New York Tribune*, December 20, 1865, and *New York Herald*, December 20, 1865.

3. *New York Tribune*, June 24, 1865.

4. *Columbian Register* (New Haven, Conn.), October 21, 1865.

5. John T. Trowbridge, *The Desolate South, 1865–1866: A Picture of the Battlefields and of the Devastated Confederacy*, ed. Gordon Carroll (Boston: Little, Brown, 1956), 41. Also see Sidney Andrews, *The South since the War*, abridged and with a new introduction by Heather Cox Richardson (Baton Rouge: Louisiana State University Press, 2004); and John Richard Dennett, *The South as It Is: 1865–1866*, ed. with an introduction by Henry M. Christman (New York: Viking, 1965).

6. House Exec. Doc. No. 11, 39th Cong., 1st sess., 45–46 (December 18, 1865). Also see Oliver Otis Howard, *Autobiography of Gen. Oliver Otis Howard: Major General United States Army, Volume Two* (New York: Baker and Taylor, 1908), 222–23.

7. *Springfield Weekly Republican*, August 12, 1865.

8. Erik L. McKitrick, *Andrew Johnson and Reconstruction* (Chicago: University of Chicago Press, 1960), 162–65. Johnson also sent O. O. Howard on a tour through the South, but this was to report on the nature of land claims by planters who had had their property confiscated during the war. The president in general overturned transfer of property to the freedpeople.

9. *Speeches, Correspondence, and Political Papers of Carl Schurz*, ed. Frederic Bancroft, 6 vols. (New York: G. P. Putnam's Sons, 1913), 1:258–59, 264 [quotation]; Paul H. Bergeron, *Andrew Johnson's Civil War and Reconstruction* (Knoxville: University of Tennessee Press, 2011), 90–91; Hans L. Trefousse, *Andrew Johnson: A Biography* (New York: Norton, 1989), 226; McKitrick, *Andrew Johnson and Reconstruction*, 162–64; George R. Bentley, *A History of the Freedmen's Bureau* (Philadelphia: University of Pennsylvania Press, 1955), 107–8.

10. *Speeches, Correspondence, and Political Papers of Carl Schurz*, 1:264–65; Beverly Wilson Palmer, ed., *The Selected Letters of Charles Sumner: Volume Two, 1859–1874* (Boston: Northeastern University Press, 1990), 339, 347.

11. Joseph H. Mahaffey, "Carl Schurz's Letters from the South," *Georgia Historical Quarterly* 35 (September 1951): 222–57.

12. "Misrepresenting the South," *Albany Argus*, July 28, 1865.

13. *Alexandria Gazette*, August 30, 1865; *Cincinnati Enquirer*, September 12, 1865.

14. John Y. Simon, ed., *The Papers of Ulysses S. Grant*, 32 vols. (Carbondale: Southern Illinois University Press, 1967–2012), 15:428–29. For accounts of Grant's tour, see Ron Chernow, *Grant* (New York: Penguin Press, 2017), 563–66; Brooks D. Simpson, "Grant's Tour of the South Revisited," *Journal of Southern History* 54 (August 1988): 425–48; William S. McFeely, *Grant: A Biography* (New York: Norton, 1981), 238–41; Bergeron, *Andrew Johnson's Civil War*,

90–91; Trefousse, *Andrew Johnson*, 238–39; and McKitrick, *Andrew Johnson and Reconstruction*, 164–65.

15. Jean Edward Smith, *Grant* (New York: Simon and Schuster, 2001), 422.

16. *Report of the Joint Committee on Reconstruction* (Washington, D.C.: GPO, 1866), xvii.

17. "Condition of the South," Senate Exec. Doc. No. 2, 39th Cong., 1st sess., 1–2 (December 19, 1865); *New York Herald*, December 20, 1865.

18. "Condition of the South," 5, 7 (Yankees), 13 (treason).

19. "Condition of the South," 18 (italics in original), 105.

20. "Condition of the South," 107–8.

21. *Congressional Globe*, 39th Cong., 1st sess., 79 (December 19, 1865). Also see *New York Tribune*, December 20, 1865.

22. *New York Tribune*, December 20, 1865.

23. *Congressional Globe*, 92–95 (December 20, 1865).

24. *Congressional Globe*, 95–96.

25. *Cincinnati Enquirer*, February 26, 1867.

26. Carl Schurz to Wife, January 12, 1866, in *Intimate Letters of Carl Schurz, 1841–1869*, ed. Joseph Schafer (Madison: State Historical Society of Wisconsin, 1928), 356.

27. Simon, *Papers of Ulysses S. Grant*, 16:69–70.

28. Simon, 16:69–70.

29. "Condition of the South," 107.

30. "Freedmen's Bureau," House Exec. Doc. No. 70, 39th Cong., 1st sess., 230 (Fisk, emphasis in original), 201–2 (March 20, 1866).

31. "Freedmen's Bureau," 239, 202.

32. See, for instance, Circulars No. 10 and 11 of July 11 and 12, 1865, in "Freedmen's Bureau," 184–86.

33. "Freedmen's Bureau," 201–2.

34. Simon, *Papers of Ulysses S. Grant*, 16:228–29n.

35. Simon, 16:228.

36. "Murder of Union Soldiers," House Report No. 23, 39th Cong., 2nd sess., 33 (February 22, 1867).

37. *Boston Daily Advertiser*, December 22, 1866.

38. *New York Tribune*, December 25, 1866 (emphasis in original).

39. *Daily Constitutionalist* (Augusta, Ga.), October 18, 1866.

40. *Cincinnati Daily Commercial*, August 17, 1865; *Springfield Weekly Republican*, September 16, 1865 ("pestilent lies").

41. *New York Times*, August 3, 1866.

42. *New York Times*, August 14, 1866.

43. A. P. Ketchum to Each Assistant Commissioner, September 24, 1866, image 227, reel 2, M742, BRFAL, NA. Also see John A. Carpenter, *Sword and Olive Branch: Oliver Otis Howard* (Pittsburgh: University of Pittsburgh Press, 1964), 129.

44. *Journal of the Senate of the United States of America*, 39th Cong., 2nd sess., vol. 59, 77 (January 8, 1867). This resolution came on January 8, 1867. There had been an earlier inquiry from the House on December 3, in which

the Committee on the Judiciary was asked to look into a sale but then tacked on a request for the committee to see if steps had been taken by the president to enforce the law and prevent outrages. It also empowered the committee to subpoena papers and persons to report to the House on the matter. Johnson was answering both of these inquiries. *Journal of the House of Representatives*, 39th Cong., 2nd sess., vol. 64, 89 (January 11, 1867).

45. *Journal of the Senate of the United States of America*, 39th Cong., 2nd sess., vol. 59, 308 (February 19, 1867).

46. Howard K. Beale, ed., *Diary of Gideon Welles: Secretary of the Navy under Lincoln and Johnson*, 3 vols. (New York: W. W. Norton 1960), 3:44.

47. Beale, 3:42.

48. Simon, *Papers of Ulysses S. Grant*, 17:50n.

CHAPTER 2

1. John William De Forest, *A Union Officer in the Reconstruction*, ed. James H. Croushore and David Morris Potter (1948; new ed., Baton Rouge: Louisiana State University Press, 1976), 1–3. This account was originally published as "A Report of Outrages," *Harper's New Monthly Magazine*, December 1868, 75–84.

2. De Forest, 2–3. For his original report, see Records of the Assistant Commissioner for the State of South Carolina, Bureau of Refugees, Freedmen, and Abandoned Lands, image 32, reel 34, M869, RG 105, BRFAL, NA.

3. De Forest, *Union Officer in the Reconstruction*, 10.

4. De Forest, 24n, 110–11.

5. For the different assessments offered by historians, see overviews by Paul A. Cimbala, ed., *Under the Guardianship of the Nation: The Freedmen's Bureau and the Reconstruction of Georgia, 1865–1870* (Athens: University of Georgia Press, 1997), xiv–xv, 231n6; and Mary Farmer-Kaiser, *Freedwomen and the Freedmen's Bureau: Race, Gender, and Public Policy in the Age of Emancipation* (New York: Fordham University Press, 2010), 2–3.

6. See, for instance, Barry A. Crouch, "A Spirit of Lawlessness: White Violence; Texas Blacks, 1865–1868," *Journal of Social History* 18 (Winter 1984): 218. For an argument against considering bureau agents as the extension of Radicals, see John Cox and LaWanda Cox, "General O. O. Howard and the 'Misrepresented Bureau,'" *Journal of Southern History* 19 (November 1953): 437.

7. Kidada E. Williams, *They Left Great Marks on Me: African American Testimonies of Racial Violence from Emancipation to World War I* (New York: New York University Press, 2012), 5.

8. George R. Bentley, *A History of the Freedmen's Bureau* (Philadelphia: University of Pennsylvania Press, 1955), 72, 73 (quotation). An assistant commissioner in North Carolina reported in October 1865 that while the number of assistants was supposed to be thirty-three, the total manpower had never achieved higher than twenty and had at that time fifteen, or less than half the staffing needed. See "Message of the President Communicating Reports of

Assistant Commissioners of the Freedmen's Bureau," Senate Exec. Doc. No. 27, 39th Cong., 1st sess., 160 (March 5, 1866).

9. Sidney Andrews, *The South since the War*, abridged and with a new introduction by Heather Cox Richardson (Baton Rouge: Louisiana State University Press, 2004), 129–30.

10. [Illegible], Acting Assist. Adjutant General, to Davis Tillson, November 24, 1866, image 286, reel 2, M742, RG 105, BRFAL, NA.

11. John T. Trowbridge, *The Desolate South, 1865–1866: A Picture of Battlefields and of the Devastated Confederacy*, ed. Gordon Carroll (Boston: Little, Brown, 1956), 181.

12. William S. McFeely, *Yankee Stepfather: General O. O. Howard and the Freedmen* (New Haven: Yale University Press, 1968), 72–73; Farmer-Keiser, *Freedwomen and the Freedmen's Bureau*, 143–44; James Oakes, "A Failure of Vision: The Collapse of the Freedmen's Bureau Courts," *Civil War History* 25, no. 1 (1979): 67. For more on the choices for assistant commissioner and hiring by Howard, see Bentley, *History of the Freedmen's Bureau*, 56–61; and Cox and Cox, "General O. O. Howard and the 'Misrepresented Bureau,'" 431–33.

13. The full report was published in the *New York Tribune*, August 10, 1866.

14. *New York Tribune*, August 10, 1866.

15. Williams, *They Left Great Marks on Me*, 5.

16. Williams, 3–5.

17. Report of Mr. Eliot from the Committee on Freedmen's Affairs, House Report No. 30, 40th Cong., 2nd sess., 5 (March 10, 1868). The 100,000 figure was popular among supporters of the Freedmen's Bureau. O. O. Howard also adopted it in his reports. See Bentley, *History of the Freedmen's Bureau*, 152.

18. *Report of Special Committee on Lawlessness and Violence in Texas* (Austin: Daily Republican, 1868), 4, 5.

19. O. O. Howard to Gen. D. Tillson, May 7, 1866, O. O. Howard Papers, Bowdoin University.

20. Alfred L. Hough, Brevet Colonel, U.S. Army, to Brevet Major General W. D. Whipple, A.A.G., Department of Cumberland, September 10, 1868, in "Message of the President of the United States," House Exec. Doc. No. 1, 40th Cong., 3rd sess., 188 (1868).

21. O. O. Howard to Gen. D. Tillson, May 7, 1866, O. O. Howard Papers, Bowdoin University.

22. Trevor Plante of the National Archives indicated that the murders and outrages from the three missing states may be filed in another series with a different title. "Another possibility," he noted, "is that the records themselves were never transferred to NARA." As of this writing, we had not unlocked the mystery. Trevor Plante to William Blair, July 14, 2020, email in author's possession.

23. Christopher B. Bean, "A Stranger amongst Strangers: An Analysis of the Freedmen's Bureau Subassistant Commissioners in Texas, 1865–1868" (Ph.D. diss., University of North Texas, 2008), 163–65, 321.

24. Farmer-Kaiser has provided one of the more extensive examinations of child custody battles involving the Freedmen's Bureau. See her *Freedwomen and the Freedmen's Bureau,* chap. 5. Also see Eric Foner, *Reconstruction: America's Unfinished Revolution, 1863–1877* (New York: Harper and Row, 1988), 201; Kate Masur, *An Example for All the Land: Emancipation and the Struggle over Equality in Washington, D.C.* (Chapel Hill: University of North Carolina Press, 2010), 75–76; and Karin L. Zipf, "Reconstructing 'Free Woman': African-American Women, Apprenticeship, and Custody Rights during Reconstruction," *Journal of Women's History* 2 (Spring 2000): 8–31. Barbara Fields has estimated that 2,519 children in Maryland were apprenticed between November 1864 and April 1867. See her *Slavery and Freedom on the Middle Ground* (New Haven: Yale University Press, 1985), 153.

25. Basil Crowdy, his wife, and their three children, reported June 16, 1866, reel 21, M1055, RG 105, BRFAL, NA. The case is also mentioned in Farmer-Kaiser, *Freedwomen and the Freedmen's Bureau,* 114.

26. Farmer-Kaiser, *Freedwomen and the Freedmen's Bureau,* 101; Foner, *Reconstruction,* 201. For the decision, see *In re Turner,* 24 F. Cas. 337 (C. C. Md. 1867).

27. Report of the Commissioner of the Freedmen's Bureau in House Exec. Doc. No. 1, 40th Cong., 2nd sess., 659–60 (1867).

28. Hannah Rosen, *Terror in the Heart of Freedom: Citizenship, Sexual Violence, and the Meaning of Race in the Postemancipation South* (Chapel Hill: University of North Carolina Press, 2009); Jonathan W. White, "Martial Law and the Expansion of Civil Liberties during the Civil War," in *Ex Parte Milligan Reconsidered: Race and Civil Liberties from the Lincoln Administration to the War on Terror,* ed. Stewart L. Winger and Jonathan W. White (Lawrence: University Press of Kansas, 2020), 57; Crystal Feimster, "'What If I Am a Woman': Black Women's Campaigns for Sexual Justice and Citizenship," in *The World the Civil War Made,* ed. Gregory P. Downs and Kate Masur (Chapel Hill: University of North Carolina Press, 2015), 249–50, 257–58; Sharon Romeo, *Gender and the Jubilee: Black Freedom and the Reconstruction of Citizenship in Civil War Missouri* (Athens: University of Georgia Press, 2016), 1–2; Farmer-Kaiser, *Freedwomen and the Freedmen's Bureau,* 146.

29. On rape, see especially the studies of Rosen, *Terror in the Heart of Freedom;* Farmer-Kaiser, *Freedwomen and the Freedmen's Bureau,* 160–63; and Feimster, "'What If I Am a Woman,'" 249–68.

30. Farmer-Kaiser, *Freedwomen and the Freedmen's Bureau,* 161–62; Susan Gooseley in Texas Murders and Outrages, images 75–76, reel 32, M821, RG 105, BRFAL, NA.

31. Robert William Fogel and Stanley L. Engerman, *Time on the Cross: The Economics of American Negro Slavery* (Boston: Little, Brown, 1974), 132; James Ford Rhodes, *History of the United States from the Compromise of 1850 to the Final Restoration of Home Rule at the South in 1877, Vol. I, 1850–1854* (New York: Macmillan, 1910), 339–40. Also see *Population of the United States in 1860,*

Compiled from the Original Returns of the Eighth Census (Washington, D.C.: GPO, 1864), x.

32. James Riley in Tennessee Murders and Outrages, image 74, reel 34, M999; Winnie Anderson in South Carolina Murders and Outrages, image 161, reel 34, M869; Nelson Lanford in Georgia Murders and Outrages, image 374, reel 32, M798, all in RG 105, BRFAL, NA.

33. Farmer-Kaiser, *Freedwomen and the Freedmen's Bureau*, 113.

34. Texas Murders and Outrages, images 91–92 (Cautly), images 230–31 (Harrison), reel 32, M821, RG 105, BRFAL, NA.

35. Tennessee Murders and Outrages, images 35–36, reel 34, M999, RG 105, BRFAL, NA.

36. Farmer-Kaiser, *Freedwomen and the Freedmen's Bureau*, 8; Rosen, *Terror in the Heart of Freedom*, 3. For Black women's political identities as Unionists, see Thavolia Glymph, *The Women's Fight: The Civil War's Battles for Home, Freedom, and Nation* (Chapel Hill: University of North Carolina Press, 2020). Also on women's political struggles, see Stephanie McCurry, *Confederate Reckoning: Power and Politics in the Civil War South* (Cambridge, Mass.: Harvard University Press, 2010), esp. chaps. 6 and 7. For reporting crimes as resistance, see Williams, *They Left Great Marks on Me*, 3–5.

37. Reports dated February 21 and February 1, 1868, Virginia Murders and Outrages, image 29, reel 59, M1048, RG 105, BRFAL, NA. For Black female activism during the Civil War, see Judith Giesberg, *Army at Home: Women and the Civil War on the Northern Home Front* (Chapel Hill: University of North Carolina Press, 2009), chap. 4.

38. George Grafton Wilson, *Insurgency: Lectures Delivered at the Naval War College, Newport, Rhode Island* (Washington, D.C.: GPO, 1900); Colonel C. E. Callwell, *Small Wars: Their Principles and Practice*, 3rd ed. (Lincoln: University of Nebraska Press, 1996). One of the seminal studies of the subject came out just before World War II by the U.S. Marine Corps. See U.S. Marine Corps, *Small Wars Manual* (Washington, D.C.: GPO, 1940). For a good discussion of this issue, and how the federal government never quite identified resistance in the South as an insurgency, see Mark Grimsley, "Wars for the American South: The First and Second Reconstructions Considered as Insurgencies," *Civil War History* 58 (March 2012): 6–36.

39. *U.S. Government Counterinsurgency Guide* (Washington, D.C.: Bureau of Political-Military Affairs, January 2009), 2. Also see Donald W. Hamilton, *The Art of Insurgency: American Military Policy and the Failure of Strategy in Southeast Asia* (Westport, Conn.: Greenwood, 1998), 5.

40. Elaine Frantz Parsons, *Ku-Klux: The Birth of the Klan during Reconstruction* (Chapel Hill: University of North Carolina Press, 2015), 5–6.

41. Tennessee Murders and Outrages, image 87, reel 34, M999, RG 105, BRFAL, NA.

42. George D. Reynolds, to J. H. Weber, Southern District, Mississippi, November 4, 1865, image 415, reel 32, M1907, RG 105, BRFAL, NA.

43. Reports of Mary Stewart and Damascus D. Day of August 19 and 20, 1865, Louisiana Murders and Outrages, image 273, reel 34, M1027, RG 105, BRFAL, NA. Also see "The Freedmen's Bureau Online," Murders and Outrages for Louisiana, accessed December 16, 2020, https://freedmensbureau.com/louisiana/outrages/marystewart.htm.

44. Report of Mary Stewart and Damascus D. Day, August 20, 1865, Louisiana Murders and Outrages, image 273.

45. Report of June 30, 1866, Virginia Murders and Outrages, images 81–82, reel 59, M1948, RG 105, BRFAL, NA.

46. Gregory P. Downs, *After Appomattox: Military Occupation and the Ends of War* (Cambridge, Mass.: Harvard University Press, 2015).

CHAPTER 3

1. *Congressional Globe*, 39th Cong., 2nd sess., 1565 (February 19, 1867).

2. *Congressional Globe*, 1466 (quotation), 1441 (incompetence and plantations) (February 16, 1867).

3. Gregory P. Downs, *After Appomattox: Military Occupation and the Ends of War* (Cambridge, Mass.: Harvard University Press, 2015); Laura Edwards, *A Legal History of the Civil War and Reconstruction: A Nation of Rights* (New York: Cambridge University Press, 2015), 98–99; Michael Les Benedict, "Preserving the Constitution: The Conservative Basis of Radical Reconstruction," *Journal of American History* 61 (June 1974): 74–76; David S. Louk, "Reconstructing the Congressional Guarantee of Republican Government," *Vanderbilt Law Review* 73 (April 2020): 705–15.

4. *New York Herald*, December 21 and 24, 1866; *Times Picayune (New Orleans)*, December 26, 1866; *Norwich (Conn.) Aurora*, January 5, 1867; *Springfield Weekly Republican*, January 12, 1867; *The Crisis*, January 9, 1867.

5. *New York World*, December 25, 1866.

6. "Report of the Select Committee on the New Orleans Riots," House Report No. 16, 39th Cong., 2nd sess. (February 11, 1867); Gilles Vandal, "The Origins of the New Orleans Riot of 1866, Revisited," *Louisiana History: The Journal of the Louisiana Historical Association* 22 (Spring 1981): 135–65.

7. "Report of the Select Committee on the New Orleans Riots," 24.

8. "Report of the Select Committee on the New Orleans Riots," 26–27, 34.

9. Edwards, *Legal History of the Civil War*, 99. For detailed background, see Louk, "Reconstructing the Congressional Guarantee of Republican Government," 705–15; and Eric Foner, *Reconstruction: America's Unfinished Revolution, 1863–1877* (New York: Harper and Row, 1988), 232–33. Scholars who suggest that the war powers played a more important role than the guarantee clause include Downs, *After Appomattox*; and Benedict, "Preserving the Constitution," 75–76.

10. "Murder of Union Soldiers," House Report No. 23, 39th Cong., 2nd sess., 1–2 (February 22, 1867).

11. "Murder of Union Soldiers," 3–4.

12. "Murder of Union Soldiers," 5.

13. "Murder of Union Soldiers," 7–8.

14. *Detroit Tribune*, March 1, 1867.

15. *United States Statutes at Large*, 39th Cong., 2nd sess. (1867), 14:428–29; Beverly Wilson Palmer and Holly Byers Ochoa, eds., *The Selected Papers of Thaddeus Stevens*, 2 vols. (Pittsburgh: University of Pittsburgh Press, 1997–98), 2:253–54.

16. *Congressional Globe*, 1386.

17. *Congressional Globe*, 1375–76. The incidents mentioned by Wilson in the *Globe* appear in Texas Murders and Outrages, reel 32, M831, RG 105, BRFAL, NA.

18. *Flake's Weekly Galveston Bulletin*, March 6, 1867. Wilson's report is published on p. 5; the editor's comment on p. 4. Also see *Cincinnati Daily Gazette*, February 23, 1867.

19. *Cincinnati Daily Gazette*, February 23, 1867; *Flake's Weekly Galveston Bulletin*, March 6, 1867; *Washington (Pa.) Reporter*, March 6, 1867; *National Aegis*, March 9, 1867; Benjamin Burks Kendrick, *Journal of the Joint Committee of Fifteen on Reconstruction, 39th Congress, 1865–1867* (New York: Columbia University, 1914), 383.

20. *Congressional Globe*, 1377.

21. Brevet Brig. Genl. Samuel Thomas to Headquarters, March 9, 1867, Louisiana Murders and Outrages, images 269–305, 270 (quotation), reel 34, M1027, RG 105, BRFAL, NA. Also see the Freedmen's Bureau Online, accessed August 2, 2020, www.freedmensbureau.com/louisiana/outrages/outrages4.htm.

22. *Congressional Globe*, 1441.

23. *Congressional Globe*, 1466.

24. *Congressional Globe*, 1565; Kendrick, *Journal of the Joint Committee*, 383.

25. *Congressional Globe*, 1567.

26. Historian John A. Carpenter has offered a similar assessment. See his *Sword and Olive Branch: Oliver Otis Howard* (Pittsburgh: University of Pittsburgh Press, 1964), 130.

27. *Congressional Globe*, 1633.

28. See, for instance, *New York World*, March 21, 1867.

29. See, for example, the *Alexandria Gazette*, April 16, 1867 (political pilgrims); and *Macon Weekly Telegraph*, May 24, 1867 (vagabond fanatics). Speakers listed as heading into the South included Congressman William D. Kelley of Pennsylvania, Congressman Benjamin Butler of Massachusetts, and Senators James W. Nye and William M. Stewart of Nevada. For some of the African American speakers, see *Richmond Whig*, May 3, 1867.

30. Lt. J. M. Babcock to Major George D. Reynolds County of Claiborne, Port Gibson, December 20, 1865, images 621–23, reel 32, M1907, Mississippi, RG 105, BRFAL, NA. For a description of the militia danger in Mississippi, see John T. Trowbridge, *The Desolate South, 1865–1866: A Picture of the Battlefields and of the Devastated Confederacy* (Boston: Little, Brown and Company, 1956),

197–98. On militias in the South, see Carole Emberton, *Beyond Redemption: Race, Violence, and the American South after the Civil War* (Chicago: University of Chicago Press, 2013), 87–92, and her article "The Limits of Incorporation: Violence, Gun Rights, and Gun Regulation in the Reconstruction South," *Stanford Law and Policy Review* 17 (May 2006): 618–21.

31. James Thomas, Bvt. Brig. General, to the Hon. Henry Wilson, Washington, January 4, 1867, image 67, reel 3, M742, RG 105, BRFAL, NA.

32. *Congressional Globe*, 1577.

33. *Congressional Globe*, 1848, 1849. Also see Stephen P. Halbrook, *Freedmen, the Fourteenth Amendment, and the Right to Bear Arms, 1866–1876* (Westport, Conn.: Greenwood, 1998), 68–69; and Mark Wahlgren Summers, *A Dangerous Stir: Fear, Paranoia, and the Making of Reconstruction* (Chapel Hill: University of North Carolina Press, 2009), 154–55.

34. Henry Wilson, *History of the Reconstruction Measures of the Thirty-Ninth and Fortieth Congresses, 1865–68* (Hartford, Conn.: Hartford Publishing Company, 1868), 381–84.

35. For a sampling, see *New York Herald*, May 1 and May 13, 1867; *Cincinnati Daily Gazette*, May 23, 1867; *Boston Daily Advertiser*, April 6, 1867; and *New York Tribune*, April 20, 1867.

36. *Boston Daily Journal*, April 8, 1867; *Albany Evening Journal*, April 26, 1867 (apostle of moderation).

37. *Macon Weekly Telegraph*, April 26, 1867; *Richmond Whig*, April 5, 1867.

38. *Providence Evening Press*, April 15, 1867.

39. *Detroit Tribune*, May 24, 1867.

40. *New York World*, October 22, 1867.

41. Michael Les Benedict, "The Rout of Radicalism: Republicans and the Elections of 1867," *Civil War History* 18 (December 1972): 341–43; Foner, *Reconstruction*, 314–16.

42. *Evening Argus* (Rock Island, Ill.), May 15, 1867.

43. *New York World*, October 8, 1867.

44. *Columbian Register* (New Haven, Conn.), March 9, 1867.

45. The most widely circulated account by the Associated Press came from a correspondent for the *New York Herald* who sat next to Kelley during the disturbance. See *New York Herald*, May 15, 1867. Also see the *Daily National Intelligencer*, May 16, 1867. One white Southern witness wrote President Johnson that the riot was triggered by horses of the Fifteenth Infantry that became frightened and started to run through the crowd, making people think there was a riot. See Joseph H. Geiger to Dear Sir, May 15, 1867, in *The Papers of Andrew Johnson: Volume 12, February–August 1867*, ed. Paul H. Bergeron (Knoxville: University of Tennessee Press, 1994), 270–71.

46. William A. Russ Jr., "Registration and Disfranchisement under Radical Reconstruction," *Mississippi Valley Historical Review* 21 (September 1934): 176.

47. *United States Statutes at Large*, 15:2–4. The oath required the person to swear he had not voluntarily borne arms against the United States or given aid

or encouragement to the enemy. See William A. Dunning, *Essays on the Civil War and Reconstruction and Related Topics* (New York: Macmillan, 1898), 184n1.

48. Alexander Keyssar, *The Right to Vote: The Contested History of Democracy in the United States* (New York: Basic Books, 2009), 151–52; Joseph P. Harris, *Registration of Voters in the United States* (Washington, D.C.: Brookings Institution, 1929), 65–66; Richard Franklin Bensel, *The American Ballot Box in the Mid-Nineteenth Century* (New York: Cambridge University Press, 2004), 139.

49. *United States Statutes at Large*, 15:14–16; Russ, "Registration and Disfranchisement," 169–74.

50. *Message of the President of the United States and Accompanying Documents, 40th Congress, 2nd sess.* (Washington, D.C.: GPO, 1867), 24–25 (Pope), 255 (Schofield); Military Reconstruction, 40th Cong., 1st sess., House Exec. Doc. No. 20, 53 (Ord), 79 (Sheridan) (July 12, 1867). On Forsyth, see Russ, "Registration and Disfranchisement," 168–69; and Leon F. Litwack, *Been in the Storm So Long: The Aftermath of Slavery* (New York: Knopf, 1979), 546.

51. *New York Post*, April 4, 1867, quoted in Russ, "Registration and Disfranchisement," 166.

52. "Condition of Affairs in Mississippi," House Misc. Doc. No. 53, 40th Cong., 3rd sess., 114 (January 6, 1869).

53. Keyssar, *Right to Vote*, 104; Mark Wahlgren Summers, *The Ordeal of the Reunion: A New History of Reconstruction* (Chapel Hill: University of North Carolina Press, 2014), 10. On the interpretations of conservatives and Radicals, see Russ, "Registration and Disfranchisement," 176. For an exemplary presentation of registration and voting analysis, see Dale Baum, *The Shattering of Texas Unionism: Politics in the Lone Star State during the Civil War Era* (Baton Rouge: Louisiana State University Press, 1998), 172–73.

54. "Letter of the General of the Army," Senate Exec. Doc. No. 53, 40th Cong., 2nd sess. (May 13, 1868); Russ, "Registration and Disfranchisement," 179. James Ford Rhodes also used these figures in his *History of the United States: From the Compromise of 1850 to the Final Restoration of Home Rule at the South in 1877, Vol. VI* (New York: Macmillan, 1910), 82–83.

55. Russ, "Registration and Disfranchisement," 179; Rhodes estimated 150,000 disenfranchised in his *History of the United States . . . Vol. VI*, 328–29. For the 75,000 figure, see *Daily National Intelligencer*, August 2, 1867. On voting totals for the 1860 election, see Walter Dean Burnham, *Presidential Ballots, 1836–1892* (Baltimore: Johns Hopkins Press, 1955), 247–57.

56. Foner, *Reconstruction*, 316–33.

57. John W. Burgess, *Reconstruction and the Constitution, 1866–1876* (New York: Charles Scribner's Sons, 1905), 114 (exaggerated suspicions), 134.

58. *Charleston Courier*, May 2, 1867.

59. *Pittsfield (Mass.) Sun*, August 15, 1867.

60. *Pittsfield Sun*, May 16, 1867; *New York Herald*, October 29, 1867.

61. Baum, *Shattering of Texas Unionism*, 162–63; Murders and Outrages for South Carolina, image 175, reel 34, M869, RG 105, BFRAL, NA.

62. House Exec. Doc. No. 278, 40th Cong., 2nd sess., 31–32 (May 4, 1868).

CHAPTER 4

1. Louisiana Murders and Outrages, images 362, 334, reel 34, M1027, RG 105, BRFAL, NA. On Bossier, see Gilles Vandal, *Rethinking Southern Violence: Homicides in Post–Civil War Louisiana, 1866–1884* (Columbus: Ohio State University Press, 2000).

2. The violence prompted the creation of investigatory bodies by the Louisiana State Assembly and the U.S. Congress to report on conditions within the state. For a list of government reports, see Gilles Vandal, "The Policy of Violence in Caddo Parish, 1865–1884," *Louisiana History: The Journal of the Louisiana Historical Association* 32 (Spring 1991): 161–62.

3. Although known by scholars, the massacre of African Americans in Louisiana has gained more attention in local histories and state journals. Historians of Reconstruction more typically fill out a list of "riots"—meaning massacres of Black people—with what happened in New Orleans (1866, 1868, and 1874) and St. Landry's Parish in 1868 and especially with the Colfax confrontation in 1873, in which armed sides fought each other military-style. One of the Dunning School monographs referenced Bossier and Caddo but, as typical of the era, claimed that carpetbaggers from the North incited Black resistance, which prompted the massacre. See John Rose Ficklen, *History of Reconstruction in Louisiana, through 1868* (1910; repr., Gloucester, Mass.: Peter Smith, 1966), chap. 11. The massacre also appeared in a brief recap of violence in Louisiana in W. E. B. Du Bois's *Black Reconstruction in America, 1860–1880*, with an introduction by David Levering Lewis (1935; repr., New York: Free Press, 1998), 681. By the middle to late twentieth century, the massacres in the Red River region were no longer as prominent a part of larger histories of Reconstruction, although the incidents were mentioned in studies of violence beginning in the 1970s. See, for instance, Allen W. Trelease, *White Terror: The Ku Klux Klan Conspiracy and Southern Reconstruction* (New York: Harper and Row, 1971), 130; and George C. Rable, *But There Was No Peace: The Role of Violence in the Politics of Reconstruction* (Athens: University of Georgia Press, 1984), 85. More recently, Steven Hahn alluded to the violence in Caddo in his *Nation under Our Feet: Black Political Struggles in the Rural South from Slavery to the Great Migration* (Cambridge, Mass.: Harvard University Press, 2003), 286–87. For the most part, what happened in the cotton fields of rural Louisiana and other parts of the non-urban South receive their due primarily because of the energies of local historians and scholars of regional studies who keep this memory alive. See, for example, Vandal, *Rethinking Southern Violence*, 23, and his articles "The Policy of Violence in Caddo Parish, 1865–1884," 159–82, and

"'Bloody Caddo': White Violence against Blacks in a Louisiana Parish, 1865–1876," *Journal of Social History* 25 (Winter 1991): 373–88.

4. *Supplemental Report of the Joint Committee of the General Assembly of Louisiana on the Conduct of the Late Elections, and the Condition of Peace and Good Order in the State* (New Orleans: A. L. Lee, 1869), xxix.

5. Carole Emberton, *Beyond Redemption: Race, Violence, and the American South after the Civil War* (Chicago: University of Chicago Press, 2013).

6. This supports the interpretation of a stockade state, or a collection of military and civilian outposts with limited reach often described by geography, in Gregory P. Downs and Kate Masur, "Echoes of War: Rethinking Post–Civil War Governance and Politics," in *The World the Civil War Made*, ed. Gregory P. Downs and Kate Masur (Chapel Hill: University of North Carolina Press, 2015), 6–11.

7. Elaine Frantz Parsons, "Klan Skepticism and Denial in Reconstruction-Era Public Discourse," *Journal of Southern History* 77 (February 2011): 53–90.

8. E. Merton Coulter, *The Civil War and Readjustment in Kentucky* (Chapel Hill: University of North Carolina Press, 1926); Anne E. Marshall, *Creating a Confederate Kentucky: The Lost Cause and Civil War Memory in a Border State* (Chapel Hill: University of North Carolina Press, 2010).

9. "Freedmen's Affairs in Kentucky and Tennessee," House Exec. Doc. No. 329, 40th Cong., 2nd sess. (July 8, 1868).

10. For the resolution, see *Congressional Globe*, 40th Cong., 2nd sess., 3658 (1868); the report is "Freedmen's Affairs in Kentucky and Tennessee," 28 (quotation). Also see Trelease, *White Terror*, 42–43.

11. "Freedmen's Affairs in Kentucky and Tennessee," 35–36.

12. Alfred L. Hough, Brevet Colonel, U.S. Army, to Brevet Major General W. D. Whipple, A.A.G., Department of Cumberland, September 10, 1868, in "Message of the President of the United States," House Exec. Doc. No. 1, 40th Cong., 3rd sess., 188 (1868).

13. "Message of the President of the United States," 717–24.

14. "Message of the President of the United States," 717–24.

15. "Message of the President of the United States," 191–92.

16. "Message of the President of the United States," 178.

17. *Message of the President of the United States and Accompanying Documents, to the Two Houses of Congress, at the Commencement of the Third Session of the Fortieth Congress* (Washington, D.C.: GPO, 1868), 1016–58.

18. *Message of the President of the United States and Accompanying Documents*, 1036.

19. *Daily Eastern Argus* (Portland, Maine), February 27, 1868. On Union Leagues, see Eric Foner, *Reconstruction: America's Unfinished Revolution, 1863–1877* (New York: Harper and Row, 1988), 283–85.

20. *New York Herald*, April 10, 1868; *Daily Albany Argus*, October 10, 1868. Also see *The Crisis*, August 19, 1868, for the allegation that secret organizations existed among African Americans that allowed them to perpetrate outrages.

21. *Daily Eastern Argus*, February 27, 1868. For the report, see "Murder of Union Soldiers," House Report No. 23, 39th Cong., 2nd sess. (1867).

22. *New York Herald*, September 1, 1868.

23. Parsons, "Klan Skepticism and Denial," 55, 61, 63.

24. Elizabeth Otto Daniell, "The Ashburn Murder Case in Georgia Reconstruction, 1868," *Georgia Historical Quarterly* 59 (Fall 1975): 300–301; *New York Times*, April 6, 1868. For a comprehensive report on the incident and subsequent military trial, see *Major General Meade's Report on the Ashburn Murder* (Judge Advocate's Office, Headquarters Department of the South, 1868), https://books.google.com/books?id=F04TAAAAYAAJ&printsec=frontcover&source=gbs_ge_summary_r&cad=0#v=onepage&q&f=false.

25. John Y. Simon, ed., *The Papers of Ulysses S. Grant*, 32 vols. (Carbondale: Southern Illinois University Press, 1967–2012), 18:213–16.

26. Daniell, "Ashburn Murder Case," 309–10.

27. Daniell, 306–9; Simon, *Papers of Ulysses S. Grant*, 18:227–32; George Gordon Meade, *Report of Major General Meade's Military Operations and Administration of Civil Affairs in the Third Military District and Dept. of the South* (Atlanta: Department of the South, 1868), 34–35. One of the earliest histories of the events proclaimed the accused innocent and called the trial "a mockery of military government." See I. W. Avery, *The History of the State of Georgia from 1850 to 1881* (New York: Brown and Derby, 1881), 387–88. For a Northern negative view of the trial as a "hateful despotism," see *Harrisburg (Pa.) Weekly Patriot*, June 25, 1868.

28. C. Mildred Thompson, *Reconstruction in Georgia: Economic, Social, Political, 1865–1872* (1915; repr., Gloucester, Mass.: Peter Smith, 1964), 285.

29. Georgia Murders and Outrages, reel 32, M798, RG 105, BRFAL, NA.

30. Georgia Murders and Outrages, image 419, reel 32.

31. Thompson, *Reconstruction in Georgia*, 287–88.

32. For the cataloging of the massacre by Freedmen's Bureau officers, see Georgia Murders and Outrages, images 417–18, reel 32, M798, RG 105, BRFAL, NA.

33. Thompson, *Reconstruction in Georgia*, 212–14; Georgia Constitution of 1868, Article III, sec. 3.3, specified no color requirement for holding office; Lee W. Formwalt, "The Camilla Massacre of 1868: Racial Violence as Political Propaganda," *Georgia Historical Quarterly* 71 (Fall 1987): 401.

34. John M. Matthews, "Negro Republicans in the Reconstruction of Georgia," *Georgia Historical Quarterly* 60 (Summer 1976): 152–53.

35. Meade, *Report of . . . Affairs in the Third Military District and Dept. of the South*, 82–83; Formwalt, "Camilla Massacre of 1868," 408–12.

36. Meade, *Report of . . . Affairs in the Third Military District and Dept. of the South*, 83; Formwalt, "Camilla Massacre of 1868," 412–14. For a summary of the slayings, see the report of Brevet Maj. O. H. Howard, November 15, 1868, in "Condition of Affairs in Georgia," House Misc. Doc. No. 52, 40th Cong., 3rd sess., 128 (1869).

37. "Condition of Affairs in Georgia," 11 (quotation); *Macon Weekly Telegraph*, October 9, 1868.

38. "Condition of Affairs in Georgia," 91–94.

39. "Condition of Affairs in Georgia," 93–94, 97, 124–39 (summaries of murders and outrages). Also see Lee W. Formwalt, ed., "Petitioning Congress for Protection: A Black View of Reconstruction at the Local Level," *Georgia Historical Quarterly* 73 (Summer 1989): 305–22. For another example of the use of Freedmen's Bureau reports by African Americans, see the *Christian Recorder*, October 3, 1868.

40. Susan E. O'Donovan, "Nelson Tift," *New Georgia Encyclopedia*, online, accessed July 15, 2019, www.georgiaencyclopedia.org/articles/ history-archaeology/nelson-tift-1810-1891.

41. For Tift's effort and the responses, see "Condition of Affairs in Georgia," 140–36, 153–54 (judge's quotation).

42. Thompson, *Reconstruction in Georgia*, 258.

43. "Use of the Army in Certain of the Southern States," House Exec. Doc. No. 30, 44th Cong., 2nd sess., 212–13, 291–92 (1877); *Supplemental Report of the Joint Committee of the General Assembly of Louisiana*, 27. Also see Vandal, *Rethinking Southern Violence*, 67; and Carin Peller-Semmens, "Unreconstruction: Slavery and Emancipation on Louisiana's Red River, 1820–1880" (Ph.D. diss., University of Sussex, 2016), 160–61.

44. "Use of the Army in Certain of the Southern States," 291.

45. "Use of the Army in Certain of the Southern States," 205.

46. "Use of the Army in Certain of the Southern States," 467 (burned victim), 213 (holes in ground).

47. Mark Leon De Vries, "Between Equal Justice and Racial Terror: Freedpeople and the District Court of DeSoto Parish during Reconstruction," *Louisiana History: The Journal of the Louisiana Historical Association* 56 (Summer 2015): 263–65.

48. *Supplemental Report of the Joint Committee of the General Assembly of Louisiana*, iv. For Hatch's recapitulation, see pp. 255–70. For the first report that came out before the massacres, see *Report of the Joint Committee of the General Assembly of Louisiana on the Conduct of the Late Elections, and the Condition of Peace and Order in the State* (New Orleans: A. L. Lee, 1868).

49. Vandal, *Rethinking Southern Violence*, 10, 67.

50. Vandal, "Policy of Violence in Caddo Parish," 177.

51. *Supplemental Report of the Joint Committee of the General Assembly of Louisiana*, xi–xiii; Melinda Meek Hennessey, "Race and Violence in Reconstruction New Orleans: The 1868 Riot," *Louisiana History: The Journal of the Louisiana Historical Association* 20 (Winter 1979): 77–91.

52. *Supplemental Report of the Joint Committee of the General Assembly of Louisiana*, xiv–xv; Carolyn E. DeLatte, "The St. Landry Riot: A Forgotten Incident of Reconstruction Violence," *Louisiana History: The Journal of the Louisiana Historical Association* 17 (Winter 1976): 41–49. For Bentley's testimony, see "Use of the Army in Certain of the Southern States," 183–84. A good recent examination of the events can be found in Matthew Christensen,

"The 1868 St. Landry Massacre: Reconstruction's Deadliest Episode of Violence" (MA thesis, University of Wisconsin-Milwaukee, 2012), 49–62.

53. *Daily Missouri Democrat,* November 4, 1868; *Cincinnati Daily Enquirer,* November 5, 1868. Also see testimony in *Supplemental Report of the Joint Committee of the General Assembly of Louisiana,* 49–53.

54. "Message of the President of the United States," House Exec. Doc. No. 1, 40th Cong., 3rd sess., xix–xx (1868).

55. *New York Tribune,* October 22, 1868; *Cincinnati Daily Gazette,* October 28, 1868.

56. *New York Herald,* September 7, 1868.

57. *New York Tribune,* November 3, 1868.

58. *Connecticut Courant,* November 21, 1868. The opposition paper was the *Hartford Times.*

59. *Supplemental Report of the Joint Committee of the General Assembly of Louisiana,* xl.

60. *Congressional Record,* 44th Cong., 2nd sess., vol. 5, pt. 1, 50–54 (positioning of troops), 69–70 (election report) (1877).

61. *Congressional Record,* 112.

62. "Use of the Army in Certain of the Southern States."

63. "Use of the Army in Certain of the Southern States," 459–70.

CHAPTER 5

1. *The Independent* (Houston), April 19, 1866; *Idaho Tri-Weekly Statesman* (Boise), May 17, 1866; *New Hampshire Patriot and Gazette* (Concord), April 25, 1866; William L. Richter, "General Phil Sheridan, the Historians, and Reconstruction," *Civil War History* 33 (June 1987): 150–51. For his repartee with a Texas newspaper, see *Daily Arkansas Gazette* (Little Rock), September 25, 1866. Sheridan was fond of remembering the incident, and one of the most repeated citations of this quotation was printed decades later in the *Washington Post,* December 19, 1883. Accounts vary as to whether he said, "Live at the other place" or "Live in hell."

2. *Report of the Special Committee on Lawlessness and Violence in Texas* (Austin: Daily Republican, 1868), 4. Also see Senate Misc. Doc. No. 109, 40th Cong., 2nd sess. (1868).

3. Randolph B. Campbell, *Gone to Texas: A History of the Lone Star State* (New York: Oxford University Press, 2003), 207; Donald E. Reynolds, *Texas Terror: The Slave Insurrection Panic of 1860 and the Secession of the Lower South* (Baton Rouge: Louisiana State University Press, 2007), 8. The problem of scale embodies the idea of a stockade state advanced by the editors of a recent study of the postwar world. The phrase describes a collection of military posts whose effectiveness was limited by geography. See Gregory P. Downs and Kate Masur, "Echoes of War: Rethinking Post–Civil War Governance and Politics," in *The*

World the Civil War Made, ed. Gregory P. Downs and Kate Masur (Chapel Hill: University of North Carolina Press, 2015), 6–11.

4. For years historians of Texas characterized the violence as typical for an underdeveloped region with a sizable frontier. For instance, Charles W. Ramsdell attributed the murderous atmosphere to "turbulent characters" in a frontier population with an absence of peace officers. Native Americans, according to him, added to the instability. See his *Reconstruction in Texas* (New York: Longmans, Green, and Company, 1910), 23, 67, 82–84. Even after World War II, E. Merton Coulter continued to write off outrages as having no connection to the politics of the war but "represented the growing pains of a frontier region inadequately policed and still encumbered by its Indians." See his book *The South during Reconstruction, 1865–1877* (Baton Rouge: Louisiana State University Press, 1947), 116–17. More recently, revisionists have offered a more complex view that accepts the reality of racial violence but debates whether to privilege the outrages as political in nature or as involving economic and social strife. For good overviews of this historiography, see Gregg Cantrell, "Racial Violence and Reconstruction Politics in Texas, 1867–1868," *Southwestern Historical Quarterly* 93 (January 1990): 333–55; and Kenneth W. Howell's introduction to his edited volume *Still the Arena of Civil War: Violence and Turmoil in Reconstruction Texas, 1865–1874* (Denton: University of North Texas Press, 2012).

5. For the strongest articulation of this interpretation, see Cantrell, "Racial Violence and Reconstruction Politics."

6. On the African-born illegals, see Sean Kelley, "Blackbirders and Bozales: African-Born Slaves on the Lower Brazos River of Texas in the Nineteenth Century," *Civil War History* 54 (December 2008): 406–23.

7. Campbell, *Gone to Texas*, 100, 110, 113; Carl H. Moneyhon, "The Democratic Party, the Ku Klux Klan, and the Politics of Fear," in Howell, *Still the Arena of Civil War*, 253, 393, 405 (estimate of Black people killed). The six counties included Brazos, Grimes, Washington, Austin, Fort Bend, and Brazoria.

8. The pattern for violence has been taken primarily from the Texas Murders and Outrages, reel 32, M821, RG 105, BRFAL, NA. Statistics existed for sixty counties in *Report of the Special Committee on Lawlessness and Violence in Texas*, 3. For more recent historians who chart the regions of violence, see James M. Smallwood, Barry A. Crouch, and Larry Peacock, *Murder and Mayhem: The War of Reconstruction in Texas* (College Station: Texas A&M University Press, 2003); Christopher B. Bean, "A Stranger amongst Strangers: An Analysis of the Freedmen's Bureau Subassistant Commissioners in Texas, 1865–1868" (Ph.D. diss., University of North Texas, 2008), 25; and Randolph Roth, *American Homicide* (Cambridge, Mass.: Belknap Press of Harvard University Press, 2009), 333.

9. David Montejano, *Anglos and Mexicans in the Making of Texas, 1836–1986* (Austin: University of Texas Press, 1987), 25.

10. Campbell, *Gone to Texas*, 207; Dale Baum, *The Shattering of Texas Unionism: Politics in the Lone Star State during the Civil War Era* (Baton Rouge: Louisiana State University Press, 1998), 73; Richard B. McCaslin, *Tainted Breeze:*

The Great Hanging at Gainesville, Texas, 1862 (Baton Rouge: Louisiana State University Press, 1994), 9.

11. Baum, *Shattering of Texas Unionism*, 30; Reynolds, *Texas Terror*, 8–9.

12. James Marten, *Texas Divided: Loyalty and Dissent in the Lone Star State, 1856–1874* (Lexington: University Press of Kentucky, 1990), 26–27; Walter D. Kamphoefner, "New Americans or New Southerners? Unionist German Texans," in *Lone Star Unionism, Dissent, and Resistance: Other Sides of Civil War Texas*, ed. Jesus F. de la Teja (Norman: University of Oklahoma Press, 2016), 104.

13. R. L. Biesele, "The Texas State Convention of Germans in 1854," *Southwestern Historical Quarterly* 33 (April 1930): 255–57; Marten, *Texas Divided*, 27–29; *Texas State Gazette*, June 24 and July 29, 1854; *San Antonio Ledger*, June 1, 1854; *Washington Sentinel*, July 6, 1854.

14. William W. White, "The Texas Slave Insurrection of 1860," *Southwestern Historical Quarterly* 52 (January 1949): 259–85; Reynolds, *Texas Terror*; Donald E. Reynolds, "Reluctant Martyr: Anthony Bewley and the Texas Slave Insurrection Panic of 1860," *Southwestern Historical Quarterly* 96 (January 1993): 345–61; Marten, *Texas Divided*, 6–7; Campbell, *Gone to Texas*, 240.

15. Reynolds, *Texas Terror*, 54. Also see Richard M. Brown, "The American Vigilante Tradition," in *The History of Violence in America: Historical and Comparative Perspectives*, ed. Hugh D. Graham and Ted R. Gurr, 2 vols. (Washington, D.C.: GPO, 1969), 1:121–70; Marten, *Texas Divided*, 6–17.

16. Baum, *Shattering of Texas Unionism*, 42–53, 72–73; Campbell, *Gone to Texas*, 241–45.

17. Marten, *Texas Divided*.

18. McCaslin, *Tainted Breeze*, 66–94.

19. Evan Rothera, "Civil Wars and Reconstructions in America: The United States, Mexico, and Argentina, 1860–1880" (Ph.D. diss., Pennsylvania State University, 2017), 81–88.

20. McCaslin, *Tainted Breeze*, 36; Glen Sample Ely, "Gone from Texas and Trading with the Enemy: New Perspectives on Civil War West Texas," *Southwestern Historical Quarterly* 110 (April 2007): 439.

21. James Marten, "A Wearying Existence: Texas Refugees in New Orleans, 1862–1865," *Louisiana History: The Journal of the Louisiana Historical Association* 4 (Autumn 1987): 343–56.

22. Marten, *Texas Divided*, 26; Baum, *Shattering of Texas Unionism*, 179 (on postwar factionalism); Smallwood, Crouch, and Peacock, *Murder and Mayhem*, introduction.

23. Brad R. Clampitt, "The Breakup: The Collapse of the Confederate Trans-Mississippi Army in Texas, 1865," *Southwestern Historical Quarterly* 108 (April 2005): 498–534; William L. Richter, *The Army in Texas during Reconstruction, 1865–1870* (College Station: Texas A&M University Press, 1987), 13; Smallwood, Crouch, and Peacock, *Murder and Mayhem*, 10.

24. William L. Richter, "'Shoot or Get Out of the Way!': The Murder of Texas Freedmen's Bureau Agent William G. Kirkman by Cullen Baker—and

the Historians," in Howell, *Still the Arena of Civil War*, 77; Texas Murders and Outrages, images 23–24, 66–69, 107–10, 115–16, 119–20, 149–50, 174–75, 190–91, 224–25, 236–37, 274–75, reel 32, M821, RG 105, BRFAL, NA.

25. John Gorman, "Reconstruction Violence in the Lower Brazos River Valley," in Howell, *Still the Arena of Civil War*, 391.

26. Cantrell, "Racial Violence and Reconstruction Politics," 333.

27. Carl H. Moneyhon, *Texas after the Civil War: The Struggle of Reconstruction* (College Station: Texas A&M University Press, 2004), 35–36; Dale Baum, "'The Old Hero of Many Cowardly and Bloody Murders': Scalawag Gang Leader Ben Brown," in Howell, *Still the Arena of Civil War*, 188–89; Cantrell, "Racial Violence and Reconstruction Politics," 333–34.

28. Texas Constitution, article III, secs. 1 and 5, article VIII, secs. 1 and 2, article X, sec. 2, (1866); Moneyhon, *Texas after the Civil War*, 46–47.

29. Moneyhon, *Texas after the Civil War*, 38–42, 48, 50.

30. John Y. Simon, ed., *The Papers of Ulysses S. Grant*, 32 vols. (Carbondale: Southern Illinois University Press, 1967–2012), 16:325–29 (quotations on 326).

31. Richter, *Army in Texas*, 32; Smallwood, Crouch, and Peacock, *Murder and Mayhem*, 43.

32. Richter, *Army in Texas*, 32; *Cincinnati Daily Gazette*, November 3, 1866.

33. Simon, *Papers of Ulysses S. Grant*, 16:326–27.

34. *Congressional Globe*, 39th Cong., 2nd sess., 1375–76 (1867).

35. Cantrell, "Racial Violence and Reconstruction Politics," 345–47.

36. Moneyhon, *Texas after the Civil War*, 70–77.

37. Barry A. Crouch, "A Spirit of Lawlessness: White Violence; Texas Blacks, 1865–1868," *Journal of Social History* 18 (Winter 1984): 221. Crouch contended that other issues such as economic and social struggles factored into violence but that there was a correlation in atrocities visited upon Black people with the rise of their political engagement. Also see Cantrell, "Racial Violence and Reconstruction Politics," 335–37.

38. Bean, "Stranger amongst Strangers," 314–15.

39. "Affairs in Texas: Letters from Governor Pease and Hon. C. Caldwell," House Misc. Doc. No. 57, 40th Cong., 2nd sess., 2–4 (1868); Texas Murders and Outrages, images 246–47, reel 32, M821, RG 105, BRFAL, NA. Also see Randolph B. Campbell, *Grassroots Reconstruction in Texas, 1865–1880* (Baton Rouge: Louisiana State University Press, 1998), 116–17.

40. "Affairs in Texas."

41. "Communication from Governor Pease of Texas, Relative to the Troubles in That State," House Misc. Doc. No. 127, 40th Cong., 2nd sess., 4–6 (1868); "Report of the Secretary of War," House Exec. Doc. No. 1, 40th Cong., 3rd sess., 262–63 (1868). Also see *San Antonio Express*, January 20, 1868; *Dallas Herald*, January 25, 1868 (reprint of Hancock's letter); and *Sacramento Daily Union*, February 7, 1868.

42. "Communication from Governor Pease of Texas," 6–7.

43. "Communication from Governor Pease of Texas," 7–23, 23–25.

44. House Exec. Doc. No. 1, 40th Cong., 3rd sess., 263 (first quotation), 264 (second quotation) (1868).

45. House Exec. Doc. No. 1, 267.

46. *Tri-Weekly State Gazette* (Austin), January 20, 1868; *Daily National Intelligencer*, March 28, 1868; *Boston Post*, April 6, 1868; *New York World*, March 30, 1868.

47. For the report to Congress, see Senate Misc. Doc. No. 109.

48. *Report of the Special Committee on Lawlessness and Violence in Texas*, 3.

49. The supplemental report with updated figures may be found in *Journal of the Reconstruction Convention, Which Met at Austin, Texas, June 1, A.D., 1868*, 2 vols. (Austin: Tracy, Siemering and Co., 1870), 1:501. Also see Moneyhon, *Texas after the Civil War*, 93–94; and Donaly Brice, "Finding a Solution to Reconstruction Violence," in Howell, *Still the Arena of Civil War*, 190.

50. Senate Misc. Doc. No. 109, 2–3 (first quotation), 5 (indictments).

51. Senate Misc. Doc. No. 109, 3. See also *Journal of the Reconstruction Convention*, 1:500.

52. Senate Misc. Doc. No. 109, 7.

53. Ann Patton Baenziger, "The Texas State Police during Reconstruction: A Reexamination," *Southwestern Historical Quarterly* 72 (April 1969): 472.

54. Baenziger, "Texas State Police during Reconstruction," 472; *Journal of the Reconstruction Convention*, 1:677–78.

55. J. M. Smallwood, "When the Klan Rode," in Howell, *Still the Arena of War*, 214–16. Also see Cantrell, "Racial Violence and Reconstruction Politics," 349–51.

56. Reggie Browne, Amy Earhart, and Toniesha Taylor, "Millican Massacre," Omeka Project, accessed January 2, 2020, https://drive.google.com/file/d/1 orMhkRykbcnCoaghtSEGw8yScMism7XJ/view; Baum, *Shattering of Texas Unionism*, 192; Smallwood, "When the Klan Rode," 227; Texas Murders and Outrages, images 336–37, reel 32, M821, RG 105, BRFAL, NA.

57. Texas Murders and Outrages, images 816–17, reel 32, M821, BRFAL, NA; Baum, *Shattering of Texas Unionism*, 174. On the killing of bureau officers, see Bean, "Stranger amongst Strangers," 360.

58. "Report of Brevet Major General J. J. Reynolds, Commanding Fifth Military District," in *Annual Report of the Secretary of War* (Washington, D.C.: GPO, 1868), 704–5.

59. Baum, *Shattering of Texas Unionism*, 192–93; Baenziger, "Texas State Police during Reconstruction," 474.

60. Baum, "Stranger amongst Strangers," 370, 372, 373, 408.

EPILOGUE

1. For the importance of the Klan hearings, see Kidada E. Williams, *They Left Great Marks on Me: African American Testimonies of Racial Violence from Emancipation to World War I* (New York: New York University Press, 2012),

6. For the transition in lynching, see Jacqueline Jones Royster, ed., *Southern Horrors and Other Writings: The Anti-Lynching Campaign of Ida B. Wells, 1892–1900* (Boston: Bedford Books, 1997), 9–10. William D. Carrigan refers to the 1890s as a third era of lynching in which large white mobs and the claim of rape became indicative of ritualized sadism and torture. See his book *The Making of a Lynching Culture: Violence and Vigilantism in Central Texas, 1836–1916* (Urbana: University of Illinois Press, 2004), 113–14, and his article "The Strange Career of Judge Lynch: Why the Study of Lynching Needs to Be Re-focused on the Mid-Nineteenth Century," *Journal of the Civil War Era* 7 (June 2017): 293–312. While the South served as a site for a majority of the lynching violence, it also happened in the North.

2. For the abolition effort, see Ellen Gruber Garvey, "Nineteenth-Century Abolitionists and the Databases They Created," *Legacy* 27, no. 2 (2010): 357–66.

3. W. E. B. Du Bois, *The Philadelphia Negro: A Social Study, Together with a Special Report on Domestic Service by Isabel Eaton* (Philadelphia: University of Pennsylvania, 1899); Patricia Hill Collins, ed., *On Lynchings: Ida B. Wells-Barnett* (Amherst, N.Y.: Humanity Books, 2002), 17; Mia Bay, *To Tell the Truth Freely: The Life of Ida B. Wells* (New York: Hill and Wang, 2009), 211. Bay adroitly situates Wells-Barnett within "the research-based social analysis advocated within this emerging scientific field [sociology]." Also showing her connection with American sociology is Paula J. Giddings, *Ida: A Sword among Lions* (New York: HarperCollins, 2008), 347. These and other scholars correctly attribute to Wells-Barnett the use of statistics in ways that anticipated subsequent historians' work on lynching. For this see Christopher Waldrep, *Lynching in America: A History in Documents* (New York: NYU Press, 2006), 3.

4. Collins, *On Lynchings*, 65–71.

5. Collins, 42–49, 58, 64.

6. See, for instance, *Chicago Tribune*, December 30, 1883.

7. *Chicago Tribune*, December 31, 1884; January 1, 1888. For the transition from a majority white to more Black victims, see Waldrep, *Lynching in America*, 115. Carrigan noted that the *New York Times* also tracked lynching, doing so as early as the 1850s, but added that the *Tribune* was more comprehensive and influential in this practice. See "Strange Career of Judge Lynch," 297.

8. Carrigan, "Strange Career of Judge Lynch," 301; Michael J. Pfeifer, "The Origins of Postbellum Lynching: Collective Violence in Reconstruction Louisiana," *Louisiana History: The Journal of the Louisiana Historical Association* 50 (Spring 2009): 189–201; Equal Justice Initiative, "Reconstruction in America: Racial Violence after the Civil War, 1865–1876," Equal Justice Initiative, accessed August 5, 2020, https://eji.org/reports/reconstruction-in-america-overview/.

9. In 1893, Wells-Barnett wrote her friend white reformer Judge Albion W. Tourgee, asking him to supply information on violence during Reconstruction: "You are more likely than any one I know to have the statistics on the subject." See Ida B. Wells to Albion Winegar Tourgee, July 1, 1893, Chautauqua County Historical Society, New York. Even in 2000, the government held hearings on how to preserve and open up greater access. See "Freedmen's Bureau

Preservation Act: Are These Reconstruction Era Records Being Protected?," Hearing before the Subcommittee on Government Management, Information, and Technology, October 18, 2000, 106th Cong., 2nd sess. (Washington, D.C.: GPO, 2001), www.govinfo.gov/content/pkg/CHRG-106hhrg75060/html/ CHRG-106hhrg75060.htm. See Ira Berlin et al., eds., *Freedom: A Documentary History of Emancipation, 1861–1867*, series 1, vol. 3, *The Wartime Genesis of Free Labor: The Lower South* (New York: Cambridge University Press, 1990), xix. For the assessment in 1912, see Waldo Gifford Leland, "The National Archives: A Programme," *American Historical Review* 18 (October 1912): 4.

10. *Chicago Tribune*, December 31, 1893. For an earlier statement of lynching as a Southern practice, see *Chicago Tribune*, December 12, 1885. Also see W. Fitzhugh Brundage, ed., *Under Sentence of Death: Lynching in the South* (Chapel Hill: University of North Carolina Press, 1997). Today, one trend in scholarship has been to show the pervasiveness of lynching as a national phenomenon by studying its occurrence in the North. See Randall Miller, "Lynching in America: Some Context and a Few Comments," *Pennsylvania History: A Journal of Mid-Atlantic Studies* 72 (Summer 2005): 275–91; and Michael J. Pfeifer, *Rough Justice: Lynching and American Society, 1874–1947* (Urbana: University of Illinois Press, 2004).

11. *New York Herald*, August 21, 1892.

12. Other prominent Black editors included John Mitchell of the *Richmond Planet*, George Knox of the *Indianapolis Freeman*, Josephine St. Pierre Ruffin of the *Women's Era*, and columnist John Edward Bruce, who echoed the title of Wells-Barnett in his *Blood Red Record: A Review of the Horrible Lynchings and Burning of Negroes by Civilized White Men in the United States: As Taken from the Records* (Albany, N.Y.: Argus, 1901). See Rosalyn Terborg-Penn, "African-American Women's Networks in the Anti-Lynching Crusade," in *Gender, Class, Race, and Reform in the Progressive Era*, ed. Noralee Frankel and Nancy S. Dye (Lexington: University Press of Kentucky, 1991), 149.

13. *Chicago Daily Inter-Ocean*, November 29, 1893.

14. Carrigan, "Strange Career of Judge Lynch," 298. For an example, see Monroe N. Work, *Negro Year Book and Annual Encyclopedia of the Negro* (Tuskegee, Ala.: Tuskegee Institute, 1912).

15. Collins, *On Lynchings*, 65–71; Carrigan, *Making of a Lynching Culture*, 133–34. Also see, for instance, *Chicago Tribune*, December 31, 1884; and January 1 for the years 1886, 1887, 1888, 1890, 1891, 1892, and 1893.

16. James Ford Rhodes, *History of the United States: From the Compromise of 1850 to the Final Restoration of Home Rule at the South in 1877, Volume VI* (New York: Macmillan, 1910), 185; Frederic Bancroft, *A Sketch of the Negro in Politics, Especially in South Carolina and Mississippi* (New York: J. F. Pearson, 1885), 17.

17. Rhodes, *History of the United States . . . Vol. VI*, 24–25.

18. John W. Burgess, *Reconstruction and the Constitution, 1866–1876* (New York: Charles Scribner's Sons, 1905), 109–10. On the Dunning School, see John David Smith and J. Vincent Lowery, eds., *The Dunning School: Historians, Race, and the Meaning of Reconstruction* (Lexington: University Press of Kentucky, 2013).

19. William A. Dunning, *Essays on the Civil War and Reconstruction and Related Topics* (New York: Macmillan, 1898), 139–40; Rhodes, *History of the United States . . . Vol. VI*, 25–26; Annual Report of the Secretary of War, 1866, House Exec. Doc. No. 1, 39th Cong., 2nd sess., 718, 733, 735, 738, 743, 744, 747.

20. John A. Carpenter, "Atrocities in the Reconstruction Period," *Journal of Negro History* 47 (October 1962): 235–36; George R. Bentley, *A History of the Freedmen's Bureau* (Philadelphia: University of Pennsylvania Press, 1955). Carpenter gained an appreciation for the bureau's efforts through writing a biography of its leader. See his *Sword and Olive Branch: Oliver Otis Howard* (Pittsburgh: University of Pittsburgh Press, 1964). For a nod at the journal literature on Reconstruction violence that arose in the 1960s, see the bibliographic essay in George C. Rable, *But There Was No Peace: The Role of Violence in the Politics of Reconstruction* (Athens: University of Georgia Press, 1984), 250.

21. Among the first historians to consult the Freedmen's Bureau records as an accurate reporting of violence were Allen W. Trelease, *White Terror: The Ku Klux Klan Conspiracy and Southern Reconstruction* (New York: Harper and Row, 1971); Leon F. Litwack, *Been in the Storm So Long: The Aftermath of Slavery* (New York: Knopf, 1979); and Rable, *But There Was No Peace*.

22. George C. Rable, "The South and the Politics of Antilynching Legislation, 1920–1940," *Journal of Southern History* 51 (May 1985): 207. For a review of legislation, see James H. Chadbourn, *Lynching and the Law* (Chapel Hill: University of North Carolina Press, 1933).

23. Emmett Till Anti-lynching Act, NAACP website, accessed April 2, 2020, www.naacp.org/latest/emmett-till-antilynching-act/.

24. On trauma and forgetting, see Judith Lewis Herman, *Trauma and Recovery* (New York: Basic Books, 1992), 1–3. For the efforts to memorialize lynching, see the web page for the National Memorial for Peace and Justice, accessed April 2, 2020, https://museumandmemorial.eji.org/memorial.

25. Williams, *They Left Great Marks on Me*, 104.

INDEX

Note: Page numbers in italics refer to tables.

Dunning school at Columbia
University, 136, 155n3
Duval, Thomas H., 111

election day violence, 78–79
election of 1868, 81, 94, 100
election of 1876, 103
election tampering, 103–5
Eliot, Thomas D., 36–37
Ellison, Henry, 97
emancipation, 8–9, 111, 113
Equal Justice Initiative, 5, 131, 138

Fayette, Mississippi incident, 50
Fessenden, Francis, 14–15
Fifteenth Amendment, 69
Fisk, Clinton B., 20
Florida: disfranchisement and, 75;
lack of atrocities records for, 40,
58, 148n22; violence in, 91
Forsyth, George A., 73
Fortune, T. Thomas, 132–33,
135, 138
Forty-Eighters, 109
Fourteenth Amendment, 3, 13–14, 21,
71, 77, 90, 135
Fourth Reconstruction Act, 76
Freedmen and Southern Society
Project, 3–4
Freedmen's Bureau: about, 9–11;
African American complaints to,
36–37; African American women
and, 43–44; agents of, 29–31, 33–34
(see also specific agents); archives
of, 1–5, 131–32, 135, 143–44n5,
164n9; community resistance to,
49–52; credibility and, 6, 8, 15,
137; criticism of, 87–89; Dunning
and, 136–37; election day violence
and, 78–79; Georgia and, 91, 92,
93–94; inconsistencies of, 31–33,
147n8; insurgencies and, 48–50;

as investigative arm, 54; Kentucky
and, 85; Louisiana massacres and,
80–81, 97, 98–99, 103, 104; lynching
and, 129, 131–32, 134, 164n9; military
intervention and, 56, 59–61,
65; militias and, 66; personnel
problems of, 32–34, 147n8;
procedural problems of, 34–35,
148n13; record collecting by, 37–41,
38, 87, 148n22; renewal of, 25–26;
reporting on atrocities by, 19–23,
26–27; Tennessee and Kentucky
and, 83–85; Texas and, 106–9, 112,
115, 118–21, 123, 126–27, 128; violence
against agents of, 22; voting and,
54–55, 71, 77
Freedmen's Bureau archives, 1–5,
131–32, 135, 143–44n5, 164n9
Freedmen's Bureau Online, 4
Fullerton, J. S., 35–36, 40

Garnet, Henry Highland, 66
General Orders No. 40, 118–19, 121
General Orders No. 44, 22–23
Georgia: Ashburn murder in, 89–91;
Black legislators' expulsion in,
92–93, 96; disfranchisement
in, 75; Freedmen's Bureau and,
33; lynching and, 137; recorded
atrocities in, 23–24, 25, 38–39,
90–96; Republican Party and, 81,
89, 92, 95–96; restoration to the
Union of, 3, 96
German immigrants, 109
Gibson, 96–97
Gooseley, Susan, 45
Graham, John, 45
Grant, Ulysses S.: Ashburn murder
and, 90; election interference and,
104, 105; as presidential candidate,
88–89; reporting on atrocities and,
18–19, 21, 22–23, 27–28, 61, 134;